PUTTING PEOPLE AT THE HEART OF POLICY DESIGN

USING HUMAN-CENTERED DESIGN TO SERVE ALL

Jamie Munger and Rudi Van Dael

NOVEMBER 2020

ADB

ASIAN DEVELOPMENT BANK

© 2020 Asian Development Bank
6 ADB Avenue, Mandaluyong City, 1550 Metro Manila, Philippines
Tel +63 2 8632 4444; Fax +63 2 8636 2444
www.adb.org

Some rights reserved. Published in 2020.

ISBN 978-92-9262-408-8 (print); 978-92-9262-409-5 (electronic); 978-92-9262-410-1 (ebook)
Publication Stock No. TCS200281-2
DOI: http://dx.doi.org/10.22617/TCS200281-2

The views expressed in this publication are those of the authors and do not necessarily reflect the views and policies of the Asian Development Bank (ADB) or its Board of Governors or the governments they represent.

ADB does not guarantee the accuracy of the data included in this publication and accepts no responsibility for any consequence of their use. The mention of specific companies or products of manufacturers does not imply that they are endorsed or recommended by ADB in preference to others of a similar nature that are not mentioned.

By making any designation of or reference to a particular territory or geographic area, or by using the term "country" in this document, ADB does not intend to make any judgments as to the legal or other status of any territory or area.

Please contact pubsmarketing@adb.org if you have questions or comments with respect to content, or if you wish to obtain copyright permission for your intended use that does not fall within these terms, or for permission to use the ADB logo.

Corrigenda to ADB publications may be found at http://www.adb.org/publications/corrigenda.

Notes:
In this publication, "$" refers to United States dollars.

Cover design by Gato Borrero.

CONTENTS

FIGURES

FOREWORD

In 2017, a study analyzed the demand and supply for skilled labor in the maritime sector in Indonesia.* A multidisciplinary team analyzed the demand for labor in the maritime sector, the supply of labor by the maritime education system, and the effect of both on the students and their careers as seafarers. In the study, traditional quantitative economic and policy analysis research methods were integrated with qualitative human-centered design methodology. The results of the study showed that complementing the quantitative research methods with the qualitative methods provided innovative insights that would not have been uncovered using the traditional methods. This taught us that applying human-centered design methods in policy and project design can enrich our understanding of potential beneficiaries and lead to better policies and projects.

The basic premises of human-centered design, which puts beneficiaries at the heart of the design process, intuitively makes a lot of sense. However, if we are honest with ourselves, quite often it turns out to be very challenging to systematically implement this process. We tend to use quantitative data, like budget allocation figures, enrollment rates, student–teacher ratios, assessment results, tracer study outcomes, employment, and household survey results to describe the needs of our beneficiaries. This type of data provides rich information on systemic issues, but does not tell us about the aspirations, challenges, and choices that students, teachers, parents, and future employers experience while participating in the system.

---

*   Education Sector Analytical and Capacity Development Partnership (ACDP-026). 2017. *Preparing Skilled and Highly Skilled Manpower for Indonesia's Modernizing Maritime Sector.* Jakarta: ACDP. This study was part of the Education Sector Analytical and Capacity Development Partnership (ACDP). This partnership was a research facility, financed by the Government of Australia and the European Union and administered by the Asian Development Bank. It supported the Government of Indonesia in conducting demand-led policy analysis, knowledge management, and capacity building in the education sector. ACDP supported various government agencies including the Ministry of Education and Culture; the Ministry of National Development Planning; the Ministry of Research, Technology, and Higher Education; and the Ministry of Religious Affairs. From 2011 to 2017, ACDP commissioned 51 studies.

Our actual engagement with beneficiaries is usually limited to a few visits to the school where we talk with teachers, have a chat with students, and have a roundtable with future employers; usually to confirm preconceived notions that came from the quantitative analysis. Human-centered design advocates for a more open-minded approach: it puts the beneficiaries at the heart of the design process and encourages us to go into the field to gain insight before validating assumptions.

Using human-centered design is a relatively new development. Therefore, it is not yet part of the standard "toolkit" used for designing policies and projects. This publication aims to introduce human-centered design by describing its basic concepts and methods. The book consists of two main parts. Part 1 discusses the principles and methods of human-centered design and illustrates many practical examples. Part 2 presents our case study on maritime education.

We hope that policy makers and project designers, in the education sector and beyond, will be inspired by this book and in the future will try to systematically include beneficiaries in their design practice. We are convinced students, teachers, and parents will all benefit.

Ayako Inagaki
Director, Human and Social Development Division
South East Asia Department
Asian Development Bank

Brajesh Panth
Chief of Education Sector Group
Sector Advisory Service Cluster—Education Sector Group
Sustainable Development and Climate Change Department
Asian Development Bank

INTRODUCTION

Meet Wawan

Wawan grew up in the port city Balikpapan on the island of Borneo in Indonesia. He studied hard to become a maritime engineer because "it seemed interesting. I could go around Indonesia—that's not bad." He finished his 4 years of schooling and 1-year internship and passed his exams only to find that his certificate was not valid because his school had not yet been approved by one of the three ministries that oversee the maritime education system. "Indonesia is funny. Its regulations are ambiguous. I have to learn things from friends. It feels like we are left on our own. In this maritime world, we can only depend on ourselves."

Wawan's story illustrates what happens when a system has fallen out of sync with the people it intends to serve. Effects are felt at different levels, but it is the students themselves who often pay the highest price. The confusion, disappointment, and financial hardship that Wawan and his colleagues experience are all symptoms of a mismatch between the maritime education system and the people it aims to serve.

Human-Centered Design

Human-centered design is a field that puts end-users—the people who will use whatever service is in question—at the center of the design process. Applied to policy projects, it puts the intended beneficiaries at the heart of the design process.

The term "human-centered design" is sometimes used interchangeably with two practices that follow a similar process, design thinking and user-centered design.

Human-centered design originally gained popularity in the private sector with a strong focus on commercial products and services. The discipline is now applied to a wide variety of sectors, such as finance, education, and health care, and for broader purposes, such as policy design and implementation. In these new territories the practice of "designing with users" is hailed as a revolutionary advance. High-profile leaders, like Melinda Gates and Barack Obama, are lauding the methodology and incorporating it into their work.

Human-centered design gained traction in the education sector as it provides a methodology to align policy initiatives with the people at the heart of the education system: students, parents, and teachers. It was used in a study to understand how the maritime education system was responding to the demand for skilled labor in the modernizing maritime sector in Indonesia.[1] Human-centered design showed how policies affected students and their careers as seafarers. The insights gained from this study inspired us to write this book. Using human-centered design to create policies and projects improves outcomes by foregrounding the impact on intended beneficiaries.

Guides Decision-Making

Policy is implemented on a large scale, leaving little room for error. Small tweaks can disrupt the lives of millions of people. Using human-centered design early on, before committing to costly changes, confirms that investments will have the intended impact on the people who will use them.

When discussing a university improvement project, management wanted to upgrade the student activity center to increase usage. At the time, hardly anyone used the center. The main reasons were believed to be unattractive design and lack of activities—hence, the proposal to upgrade it. University management agreed that an independent team should have in-depth discussions with students on the university grounds, including the student activity center.

---

[1] Education Sector Analytical and Capacity Development Partnership (ACDP-026). 2017. *Preparing Skilled and Highly Skilled Manpower for Indonesia's Modernizing Maritime Sector.* Jakarta: ACDP.

It turned out that students simply had no time to go to the activity center because, to finance their studies, the majority of them had to work at their part-time jobs after class. This insight prevented a costly decision to invest in the student center when, no matter what the design, the students would not have had the time to enjoy it.

Adds Value to Traditional Quantitative Methods

The premise of human-centered design seems simple and logical. Who does not want to consider beneficiaries in her design work? In practice, traditional policy and project design methodologies do not start from individuals' life stories and experiences. These methodologies tend to rely on disciplines, which favor quantitative data and are based on set assumptions about how users react to certain interventions. Analysis in education starts with enrollment figures, percentage of budget spent on education, teacher–pupil ratios, or Programme for International Student Assessment (PISA) scores. These are accepted practices and lead to interventions that ask to increase budget, provide scholarships, build more schools, and appoint more teachers. However, making these interventions as successful as possible requires a deep understanding of the real priorities and needs of the end-users—students, teachers, and parents. That is where human-centered design can provide valuable insight, if applied in the correct manner.

For Policy Makers and Project Designers

This book aims to provide policy makers and project designers with suggestions and examples for using human-centered design. It will illustrate how human-centered design can be applied on a consistent basis to authentically include the end-users' perceptions in the design. We aim to show that the qualitative understanding of the end-users is at least as important as the quantitative macroanalysis and, if done properly, that they can reinforce each other, leading to more effective—and more humane—policies and projects.

For Decision Makers

Decision makers can benefit from this book by enhancing their fluency in human-centered design methods and outcomes. This expands their ability to evaluate policies and projects. Does it authentically put the beneficiaries at the heart of the process, or does it just "tick the box?"

Contents of the Book

The book consists of two main parts. Part 1 discusses the principles and methods of human-centered design. These are illustrated with many practical examples, either from the literature or from the design practice of Jamie Munger, the main author of the book.

Part 2 presents our case study on maritime education. At the request of the Government of Indonesia, the Asian Development Bank (ADB) commissioned a study titled "Preparing Skilled and Highly Skilled Manpower for Indonesia's Modernizing Maritime Sector" (footnote 1). In this study, a multidisciplinary team analyzed the demand for labor in the maritime sector, the supply of labor by the maritime education system, and the effect of both on the students and their careers as seafarers, using human-centered design along with economic and policy analysis.

We conclude the book with an overview of important lessons learned on using human-centered design and suggestions for further reading.[2]

[2] The authors would like to thank Sofwan Effendi, director of infrastructure of the Ministry of Research, Technology, and Higher Education, and his team for their support for this publication. Joel Mangahas, Sutarum Wiryono, and Fredi Munger provided valuable feedback on earlier versions of the text. We also like to acknowledge the team that was responsible for the original study on the maritime sector in 2017, which inspired this book. Harry Seldadyo Gunardi, Yan Risuandi, Amelia Hendra, Abdul Hamid, Conrad Siahaan, and Premono, were the authors while Paris Nurwardani, director of learning of the Ministry of Research, Technology, and Higher Education, guided this study.

CHAPTER 1

NAVIGATING INNOVATION CHAOS

Innovation is messy.
Organizations rely on human-centered design
to navigate this ambiguity.
This chapter introduces the framework
and the value it brings.

WHAT IS HUMAN-CENTERED DESIGN?

Human-centered design is an empathic approach to innovation. It is a way for policy makers to stay in line with human values, despite shifting trends and social currents, by putting beneficiaries at the center of the discovery and development process. The human-centered design framework integrates a broad set of practices around understanding the needs, wants, and limitations of the end-users. These insights ultimately result in solutions that are more likely to be adopted and embraced by the people who use them.

In the past decade, human-centered design—also known as design thinking—has become synonymous with the term innovation. Innovation, like anything new, is ambiguous, confusing, and sometimes painfully chaotic. Human-centered design is a creative framework for navigating the fuzzy front end of new initiatives by keeping the focus trained on the needs of the end-users. It provides a strategic North Star, bringing work streams and decision makers back to the value created for the end-user.

Figure 1: Benefits of Human-Centered Design

These are the four types of value that human-centered design brings to decision-making.

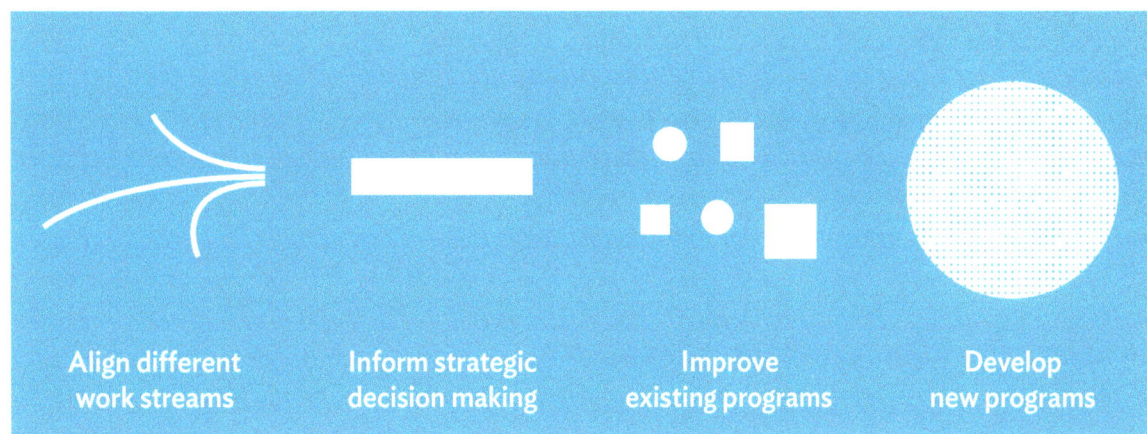

| Align different work streams | Inform strategic decision making | Improve existing programs | Develop new programs |

Source: Jamie Munger.

Shifting Focus from the Organization to the End-User

Human-centered design is sometimes called user-centered design or even people-centered design. These terms challenge organizations to change their frame of reference. Organizations tend to define people through the interactions they have with their products and services. Terms like "customer," "patient," or "passenger" define people from the perspective of the organization. Switching lenses to the end-users' perspective acknowledges that people have needs and motivations outside of their interactions with a product or service and reveals to organizations a new definition of their value and role.

Identifying the Right Problem to Solve

Seeing situations from the human's perspective (not the organization's) reveals a brand-new understanding of the problem needing a better solution. Identifying the right problem to solve is a crucial step toward knowing how to successfully address it.

To frame problems, human-centered design depends primarily on qualitative insights. These are gleaned from in-depth interviews, observations, and creative activities with end-users. Insights reflecting the individuals' realities, drawn from qualitative research, will reveal unexpected connections. They describe tensions between what people aspire toward and what they are constrained by.

Insights are a way to understand a problem in a new light. This new frame of reference leads organizations to develop more effective solutions that improve situations for their end-users.

Developing new insights requires new ways of thinking. Human-centered design has a wide variety of methods and frameworks for looking at people and situations in new ways. One of these is the "quad four" framework, developed by Kim Erwin, which offers four distinct lenses through which to look at situations: activities, ambitions, anxieties, and attitudes. These lenses cover a meaningful range of human factors— cognitive, behavioral, and emotional—to see people and situations holistically.[3]

Delivering on the Bottom Line

The world's leading technology companies, health-care providers, and financial institutions have built human-centered design into their way of doing business. The framework of designing with users was embraced first by the private sector and now increasingly by the public and social sectors as well.

---

[3]   K. Erwin. 2013. *Communicating the New: Methods to Shape and Accelerate Innovation.* Hoboken: Wiley.

Why Is That?

In the private sector, where the bottom line is revenue and shareholder value, designing with and for end-users helps business build stronger brands, differentiated products, better customer experiences, and higher customer engagement. All of these outcomes translate into monetizable value toward the bottom line.[4]

Delivering on Policy Objectives

In the public sector, the bottom line is about achieving policy objectives. Policy is made for the benefit of millions of people, yet its impact is not one-size-fits-all. In complex systems, the best intentions can lead to unintended consequences for citizens.

Human-centered design provides a greater understanding of how citizens experience policies and government services by developing insights about their pain points, aspirations, and behaviors. It informs decision makers about the needs and experiences of their constituents. Prioritizing these insights, rather than relying on those of a detached expert, helps to steer policy toward more human solutions.

Policy can be interpreted and implemented at the service level in ways that are not necessarily aligned with the underlying intent. During implementation, human-centered design aligns policy objectives with the ways people experience them through services and programs.

---

[4]   For more on this topic, see L. Keeley, R. Pikkel, H. Walters, and B. Quinn. 2013. *Ten Types of Innovation: The Discipline of Building Breakthroughs.* Hoboken: Wiley.

Figure 2: The Four As

Kim Erwin developed the Quad Four Framework, which offers four distinct lenses through which to look at situations.

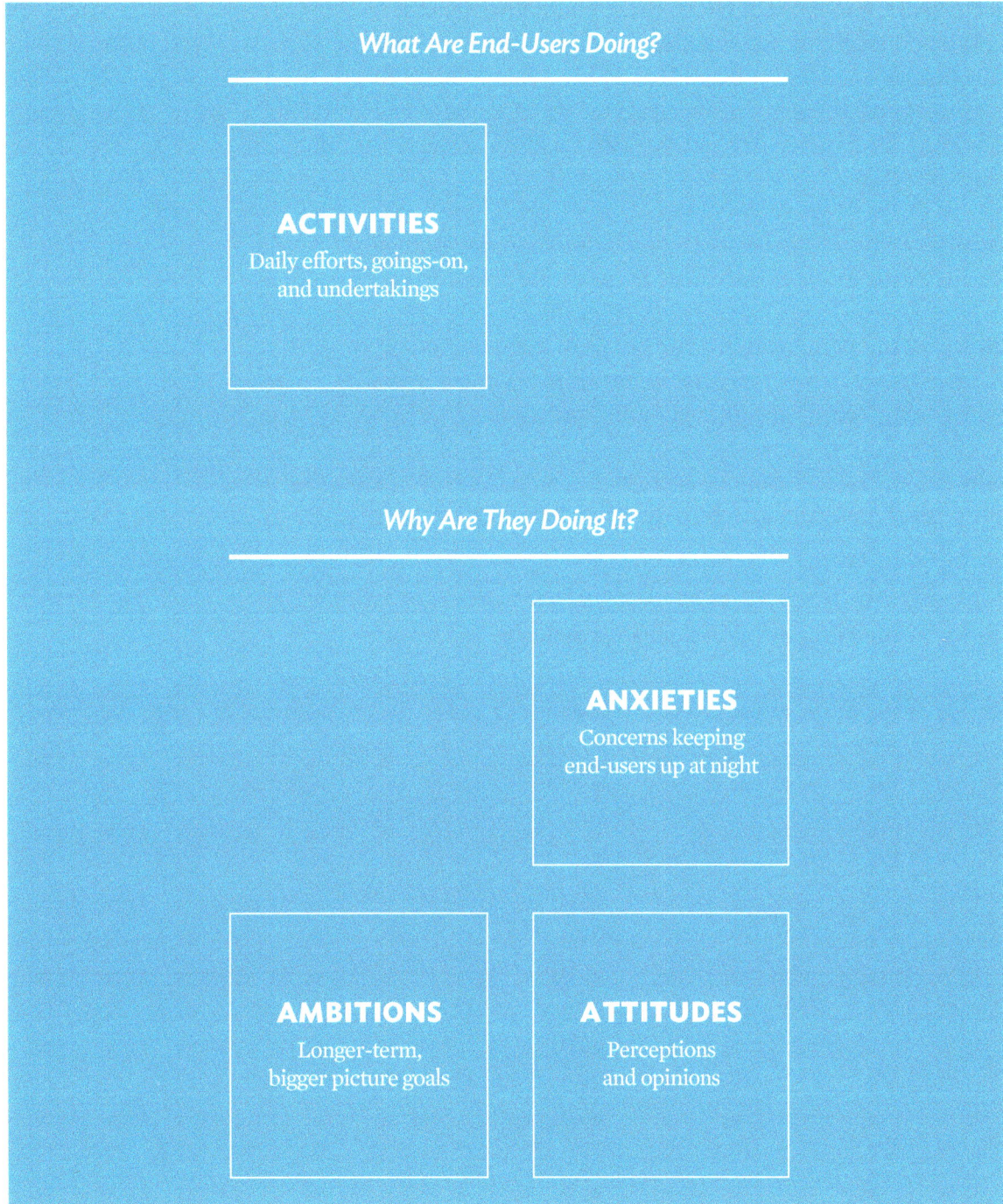

What Are End-Users Doing?

ACTIVITIES
Daily efforts, goings-on,
and undertakings

Why Are They Doing It?

ANXIETIES
Concerns keeping
end-users up at night

AMBITIONS
Longer-term,
bigger picture goals

ATTITUDES
Perceptions
and opinions

Source: Jamie Munger, based on the Quad Four Framework as found in K. Erwin. 2013. *Communicating the New: Methods to Shape and Accelerate Innovation.* Hoboken: Wiley.

Making a Case for Change

Creating value for people requires creating value for institutions as well. In developing new solutions, human-centered design seeks to strike a balance between three competing forces: desirability, feasibility, and viability. The solutions that emerge from a human-centered process should hit the overlap between these forces and thereby create a case for change not only through the human perspective, but also from the perspective of the organization.

Desirable: Will people use it? Does it solve existing problems? Is it trustworthy? Is it intuitive? Is it culturally appropriate?

Viable: Can the organization afford it? Will it make money? Will it be cost-effective? Will the institution, accrediting body, and governing boards approve, support, and endorse our plan?

Feasible: Can it technically be done by our organization? Does it identify roadblocks that can be overcome realistically?

Figure 3: Venn Diagram of Desirability, Feasibility, and Viability

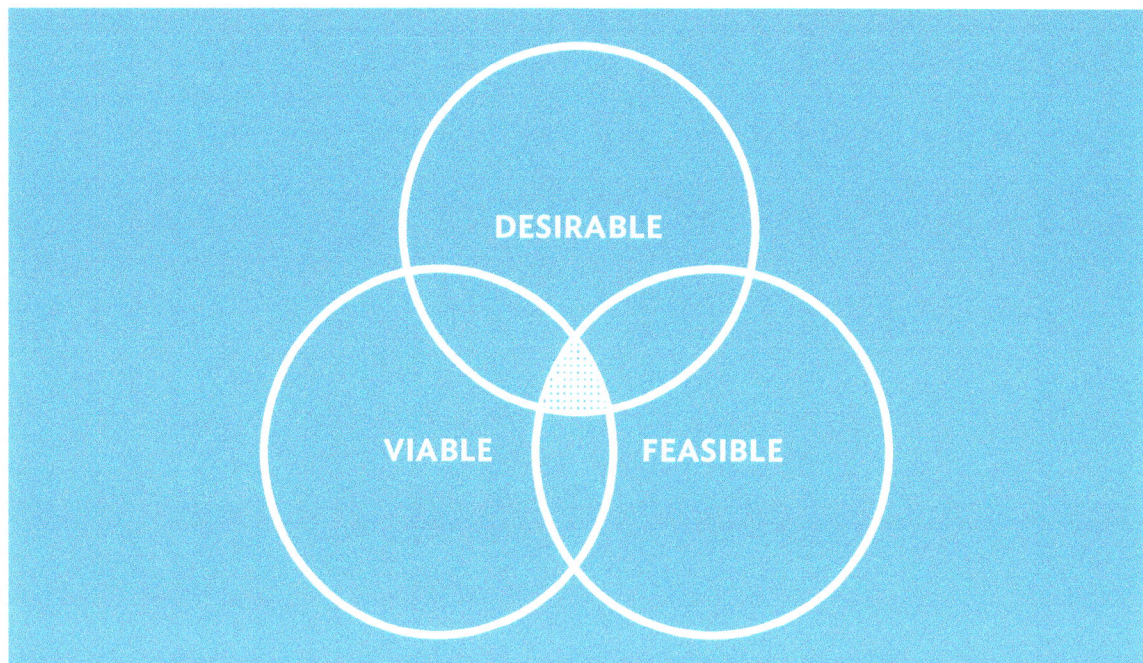

Source: Jamie Munger.

The brand was selling them something that was fundamentally at odds with their aspirations.

▲ Research with young professionals in Mumbai, India, to understand priorities for the home (photo courtesy of Emergent Design).

Many years ago, my team[a] worked with a seminal brand in India which, one generation ago, represented the very definition of high-quality items for the home, like appliances and furniture. The brand had not managed to capture the attention of the up-and-coming generation in the same way. To put it bluntly, twentysomething urbanites were not interested in buying this brand's refrigerators, sofas, bedroom sets, and washing machines.

The company suspected these new earners saw their brand as old-fashioned, something their mom and dad would buy and therefore not aspirational for young professionals living on their own for the first time. They perceived the problem to be that young people did not think their brand was cool. But did young people perceive it in the same way?

My team spent several weeks learning about twentysomething urbanites living in Mumbai by visiting their homes and talking with them about what was important, aspirational, functional, and valuable during this phase of their lives. Seeing the situation from their perspective, we learned "coolness" was not the problem. Not at all. The problem was that the brand was selling them something that was fundamentally at odds with their aspirations.

What was most important to these ambitious, young professionals was not to be "cool"—it was to be able to say "yes" to new opportunities as they arose. They prepared for this by living sparsely so, when the moment came, they would feel unconflicted about saying "yes," packing up, and moving. They compensated by sleeping on the floor instead of owning a bed, storing their clothes in cardboard boxes instead of owning a closet, and eating take out for every meal instead of owning a refrigerator and a stove.

Seeing the situation from the end-user's perspective, especially their aspirations and concerns, redefined what the brand should focus on. Rather than design a "cool" new sofa or washing machine, the team designed an innovative new service that sells, delivers, buys back, picks up, and resells secondhand furniture and appliances, thus providing some home comforts while liberating young people from the burden of ownership and the pain of moving.

---

[a] The team comprised the author, Jamie Munger; Emergent Design; and the brand staff.

CHAPTER 2

PURPOSE AND PROCESS

Human-centered design is
a philosophy and a process.
This chapter introduces both.

WHAT DEFINES HUMAN-CENTERED DESIGN?

Human-centered design is defined in two ways, by the philosophy and by process. Human-centered design does not aspire to be values-agnostic. It has a distinct purpose: to steer decision makers toward more human solutions. The result is programs, services, and products that make lives easier, healthier, and/or more fulfilling.

At the same time, human-centered design follows—and is defined by—a structured process for navigating ambiguity to arrive at meaningful and tested solutions. It offers a set of tools to decision makers that are fit for the type of complex realities they contend with. There are steps, conventions, and best practices, and these can be learned.

Empathy, Curiosity, Optimism

Human-centered design is based on three values that define why it exists, how it is practiced, and what outcomes it produces. These values, described below, are inclined toward improving situations for individuals. The ultimate aspiration of human-centered design is to build and scale positive experiences for people that organizations can sustain and benefit from. The values that underlie the practice provide practitioners with a shared foundation to rally around and a framework to evaluate their work by.

Empathy is about seeing situations from the human point of view—instead of the systemic or organizational perspective—to understand the needs and constraints of the end-users and beneficiaries.

Curiosity pushes up against static tendencies—such as confirmation bias or stereotyping—which lead back to existing knowledge rather than new insights. Curiosity is a tool for seeing complex situations in a new light rather than validating preconceived notions.

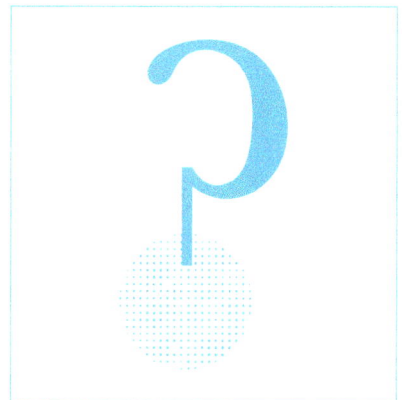

Optimism means focusing on what could be better in the future. Cynicism shuts down creative thoughts while optimism is generative. This does not mean ignoring what is painful in the present. Understanding pain points and obstacles provides valuable insight that can be leveraged as inspiration toward better solutions.

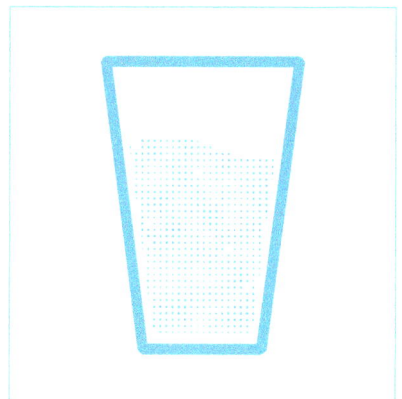

A Multistage Process for Problem-Solving

Human-centered design is a multistage problem-solving process that optimizes solutions based on a genuine understanding of end-users' needs, perceptions, and situations. Solutions that emerge make a balanced and strong case for change from both the individual and organizational perspective.

Understanding Context: Preparing to talk with users

Research: Understanding who you are designing for

Synthesis: Analyzing what you have heard into actionable insights

Prototyping: Exploring many possible solutions until the best is defined

Cycling between Exploration and Definition

The human-centered design process is applied most often at the fuzzy beginning stages of new initiatives to provide clarity and direction. Depending on the stage of the process, the objective is either to diverge or to converge. Diverging is an opportunity to expand perspectives and freely explore solutions. Converging leads to definition, prioritization, and refinement. Cycling between diverging and converging provides a structure that guards against crippling ambiguity or jumping to solutions too soon. Policies and programs reach the highest levels of refinement through repeated cycles of experimentation and testing with end-users.

Managing Risk through Experimentation

Quick, inexpensive, and strategic iterations is how solutions become increasingly tuned to the people who will need to adopt and embrace them. Iteration can have huge benefits when used to test and refine solutions before committing to expensive changes. Change can be expensive and risky. New solutions get implemented only to fail because of assumptions and flaws that went unrecognized. Inexpensive prototypes are used early in the human-centered design process to provoke feedback and reactions from key stakeholders and weed out fatal flaws.

Figure 4: Divergence, Convergence, and Iteration

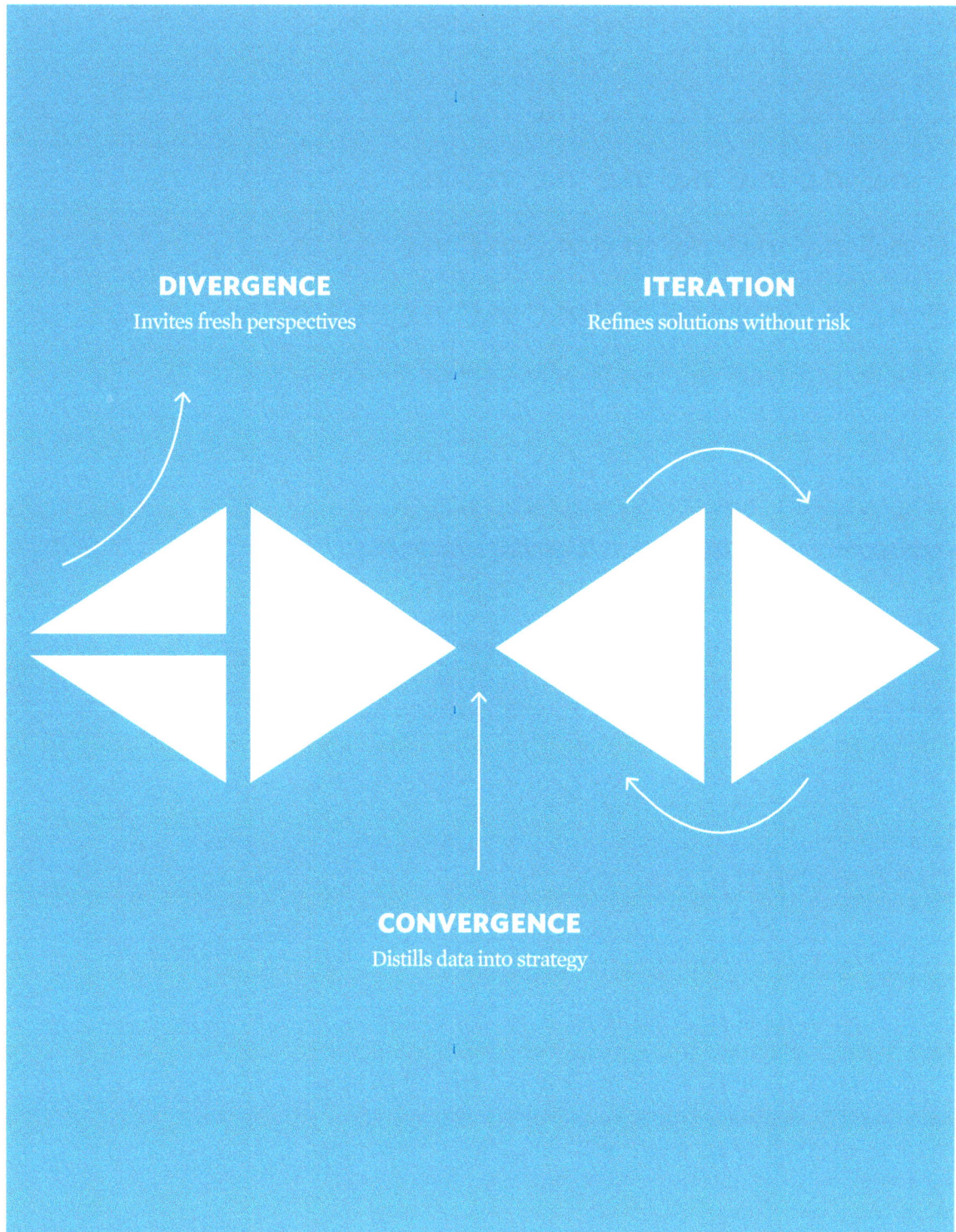

DIVERGENCE
Invites fresh perspectives

ITERATION
Refines solutions without risk

CONVERGENCE
Distills data into strategy

Source: Jamie Munger.

Adapting the framework to fit the challenge

▲ MBA students making prototypes to quickly get end-user feedback on business ideas (photo courtesy of Emergent Design).

Human-centered design is a flexible framework, not a one-size-fits-all approach. There is more than one way to use it, depending on resources, timeframes, and challenges. Below are three case studies that show three different applications.

Three-Day Workshop to Activate Existing Knowledge

An opera company was facing declining audience attendance. They wanted to deepen audience engagement by thinking holistically about the opera experience. The company had some audience research but was not sure what to do with this data. The team[a] created a map of the ideal audience experience. Through this exercise we identified an untapped opportunity. Audiences come to the theater not only for the art but also for the community. We developed thirty community-building ideas for before, during, and after opera performances. The company took over this initiative by quickly testing out ideas at the theater, identifying the most promising, and improving them from show to show.

One-Month Sprint to Arrive at One Strong Concept

A start-up wanted to help patients manage complicated medication routines. They had done research with end-users resulting in dozens of vastly different ideas for their service. Our team[a] created low-cost prototypes that addressed end-user challenges in different ways, and brought them to patients for their feedback. This sprint clarified the most important problems for the start-up to solve and guiding principles for how to solve them.

Several Month Deep Dive to Define the Opportunity

A large furniture company wanted to understand how office space can make team collaboration more effective. Their customers were big companies who invested in collaboration because it had proven to attract talent and enhance overall innovativeness. The company knew that understanding collaboration at a deeper level was going to differentiate their business in this highly competitive industry, even though they could not predict what the outcome of the project would be. For 3 months, the team[a] shadowed dozens of high-performing, collaborative teams to develop a nuanced understanding of how they work. Insights about their improvisational working style defined new opportunities to develop furniture systems that support the collective and individual needs of collaborative teams.

[a] The team comprised the author, Jamie Munger; Emergent Design; and the client's leaders.

CHAPTER 3

PROCESS DEEP DIVE

This chapter details each phase of the human-centered design process along with real-world examples of its application.

CONTEXT

Preparing to Talk with Users

The crux of human-centered design is talking with the people you are designing for. Making the most out of these in-person research moments means going in prepared with early hunches, an awareness of what knowledge already exists, and gaps that need to be filled.

Context research provides valuable perspective and topic areas to speak with end-users about. The goal is to see topics from a variety of angles: historical, economic, scientific, etc. This includes looking back at the archive of related work, looking forward for inspiration, and observing the current state of affairs.

- Create awareness of cultural and social factors
- Build off existing frameworks and theories
- Establish early hypotheses and hunches
- Develop customized research instruments

Recruit Research Participants

Human-centered design depends on insights. These come from in-depth interviews and observations with end-users and beneficiaries. When experts talk about human-centered design, they rarely discuss their strategies for finding these research participants. "Quality in, quality out"—a phrase coined in software development—describes how the caliber of inputs influences the overall result. Research participants are the inputs of human-centered design. The quality has the potential to make, or break, the final result.

Good recruiting is about finding people who satisfy two sets of criteria: fit and personality. Good recruits fit key psychographic and demographic characteristics defined by the project scope.

Figure 5: The Context Phase

The context phase is about comparing background information from different sources.

Source: Jamie Munger.

They also have personality traits making them comfortable talking about themselves, articulating opinions, telling personal stories, and reflecting out loud on decisions.

How can you tell if a person will make a good research participant? The best way is to give them a chance to express their personality, opinions, and communication style openly. This makes for a more time-consuming screening process, but a worthwhile investment in the end.

A good recruiting process might look like this:

- Use data sets to identify people who fit the right psychographic and demographic profile

- Follow up with surveys that include open-ended questions, giving potential recruits the opportunity to express themselves

- Narrow down to the top set of survey respondents and schedule a 15-minute phone call to talk one-on-one

- Select the strongest participants for the research

Expert Interviews

Subject matter experts can provide a valuable bird's-eye view of your topic. Compared to end-users who will share their personal experiences, experts provide insight on the entire landscape and examples of successes and failures. This information provides a baseline of knowledge to develop hypotheses, research activities, and criteria for finding the right kinds of research participants.

Social Listening

Observing the activity and conversations that take place online provides insight into the current state of affairs around a research topic or end-user group. Looking at blogs, websites, chat rooms, social media, and video channels reveals how people are talking about a topic, the questions they have, and the types of answers they receive. Patterns observed online can be explored in greater detail during in-person interviews.

Analogous Research

Valuable inspiration is gained from researching adjacent fields. Analogous research is the practice of looking at similar, but not directly related, topics to see a topic in a new light. Observing how other industries have solved similar challenges inspires novel applications of existing ideas.

Using Big Data

Human-centered design depends mainly on qualitative insights, but there are many ways that it can dovetail with quantitative research. Data analysis is valuable before in-person research as a means to identify research participants based on certain behaviors or preferences and identify broad patterns, hunches, and hypotheses to explore during in-person research. The mixed methods approach is gaining traction with decision makers—who had previously given greater weight to numerical data—because qualitative research provides insights about the "why" of the underlying quantitative patterns.

Figure 6: Recruiting Criteria

Expert interviews are helpful for creating nuanced psychographic profiles of the types of participants you want to interview during field research. The three profiles pictured here represent a spectrum of mentalities toward entrepreneurship. These were developed for the University of Chicago, which wanted to understand the unique experiences, considerations, and pain points of current and aspiring entrepreneurs within the academic context.

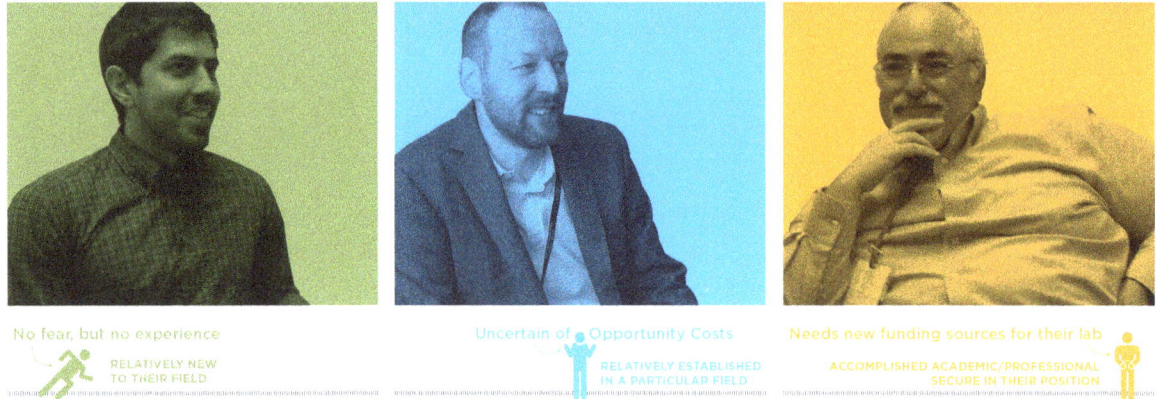

No fear, but no experience

RELATIVELY NEW
TO THEIR FIELD

Uncertain of Opportunity Costs

RELATIVELY ESTABLISHED
IN A PARTICULAR FIELD

Needs new funding sources for their lab

ACCOMPLISHED ACADEMIC/PROFESSIONAL
SECURE IN THEIR POSITION

Source: Emergent Design.

Figure 7: Research Locations

Data sets can help you identify the best places to find participants for field research. The locations shown here provide a meaningful range of urban and rural conditions while holding the other qualitative factors constant. They were developed for an outdoor product company who wanted to identify new problems to solve for women who work in physically demanding jobs.

We recruited hardworking women
in **urban and rural settings**,
each with a unique and physically
demanding job

Ray, Minnesota

Sauk Center,
Minnesota

Wheaton, Illinois

Minneapolis,
Minnesota

Source: Emergent Design.

RESEARCH

Understanding Who You Are Designing For

Human-centered design research is about getting close to end-users and hearing from them in their own words. Rather than inviting beneficiaries to off-site locations for focus groups, immersing in their individual homes, workplaces, and places of importance is the best and most efficient way to understand beneficiaries and uncover their unmet needs. This insight is the foundation for policies and programs that successfully meet those needs.

Elements of human-centered design are already present in the social and development sectors. The discipline grew from practices like participatory design and cultural anthropology, which have been central to development work for decades. Policy makers sometimes look at design thinking and wonder *what is new*?[5]

- Compare what people say, think, feel, and do
- Learn from outliers
- Understand the *why* that drives the *what* and the *how*
- Reveal unobservable mindsets and experiences

Combining Expertise to Arrive at New Insights

"Design thinking is a creative process to build up ideas. It is a different mindset to analytical thinking, which is used to break down ideas. Design thinking is more creative than traditional problem-solving approaches."[6]

---

[5]   R. Fabricant. 2014. *When Will Design Get Serious About Impact?* Stanford: Stanford Social Innovation Review.
[6]   Government of New Zealand. 2019. *The Policy Project.* Wellington: Department of the Prime Minister and Cabinet. https://dpmc.govt.nz/our-programmes/policy-project.

Figure 8: The Research Phase

The research phase is about understanding the beneficiary experience.

Source: Jamie Munger.

Human-centered design (e.g., design thinking) is particularly useful for addressing nebulous problems without an obvious answer by being more human-centric as a strategy for encouraging innovation. When applied to public programs and policy, this involves the design team collaborating with people from various backgrounds and viewpoints so insights and solutions can emerge from diverse perspectives.

Collaborators may include community leaders, funding partners, subject matter specialists, and implementing partners. Below some of the different specialties that are often included on interdisciplinary design thinking teams.[7]

Behavioral economics provides insight into the "nudges" necessary to help people make more optimal decisions.

Cultural anthropology applies social theories to facilitate a deeper understanding of why people behave the way they do.

<hr>

[7]   Design for Health. 2019. *Complementary Approaches.* https://static1.squarespace.com/static/5b0f1011b98a78f8e23aef4e/t/5b2c9da1352f53f9989f37c6/1529650594627/06+Complementary+Approaches.pdf.

Data science surfaces broad patterns in what people do and how often.

Market research contrasts and compares products and services to paint a picture of what does and does not work in a market.

Participatory design involves all stakeholders in an envisioning process to generate buy-in.

Human-centered design views problems through the end-users' perspective to develop solutions to address their needs.

Ethnographic Interviews

Human-centered design has adapted a technique of in situ research from ethnography, a branch of anthropology that involves trying to "get inside" the way a group of people sees the world. The goal is to see behaviors and choices on their terms.

Interviews take place in context—at the subject's home, work, or a relevant location—so the researchers can get a richer picture of the person and their life. Conversations are semi-structured: the researchers have specific topics they want to cover but, unlike conducting a survey, they ask open-ended questions to understand not just what people think and feel, but also—most importantly—why. Ethnography takes into account psychology, culture, and personal stories in a way that makes it distinct from other fields.[8]

---

[8]   K. Anderson. 2009. Ethnographic Research: A Key to Strategy. *Harvard Business Review*. Vol. 87–3, March Issue. https://hbr.org/2009/03/ethnographic-research-a-key-to-strategy.

Experience Maps

An experience map (also sometimes called the user journey) is a visual aid that helps people describe and illustrate important moments of an experience that stretches over a length of time. These maps surface the stages people go through, their highs and lows, and the resources they need. Experience maps are used in two ways: as a diagnostic for an existing experience, or as a brainstorming tool to visualize what an ideal experience could look like.

Sacrificial Concepts

Researchers often bring early hunches and hypotheses into the field. Rather than seek validation for these ideas, their goal is to stimulate deeper conversation and reflection from the users. These sacrificial concepts are simple, unrefined—sometimes wild—ideas that are roughly visualized with the intention to provoke discussion. Rather than just talking about an idea, having a visual artifact prompts a more specific reaction. As the name suggests, sacrificial concepts are meant to be tossed out. Their purpose is reflection, not validation. To make sure participants feel comfortable disliking or disagreeing, the concepts should be rough, implying they are subject to change.

Cultural Probes

These are interactive activities for understanding the underlying perceptions and attitudes that influence the decisions people make. Cultural probes are helpful for externalizing thoughts that are deeply embedded, fast moving, or difficult to articulate. A simple but thought-provoking activity or game gives the participant a framework to organize their thoughts and time to reflect on their answers.

Figure 9: Biking Journeys

What are the steps people take to learn about biking? Where are the fall-off points when people give up? To answer these questions, our team used experience maps. We visited four locations and had 20 people draw a map of their biking journey in their own words, paying special attention to the high and low points.

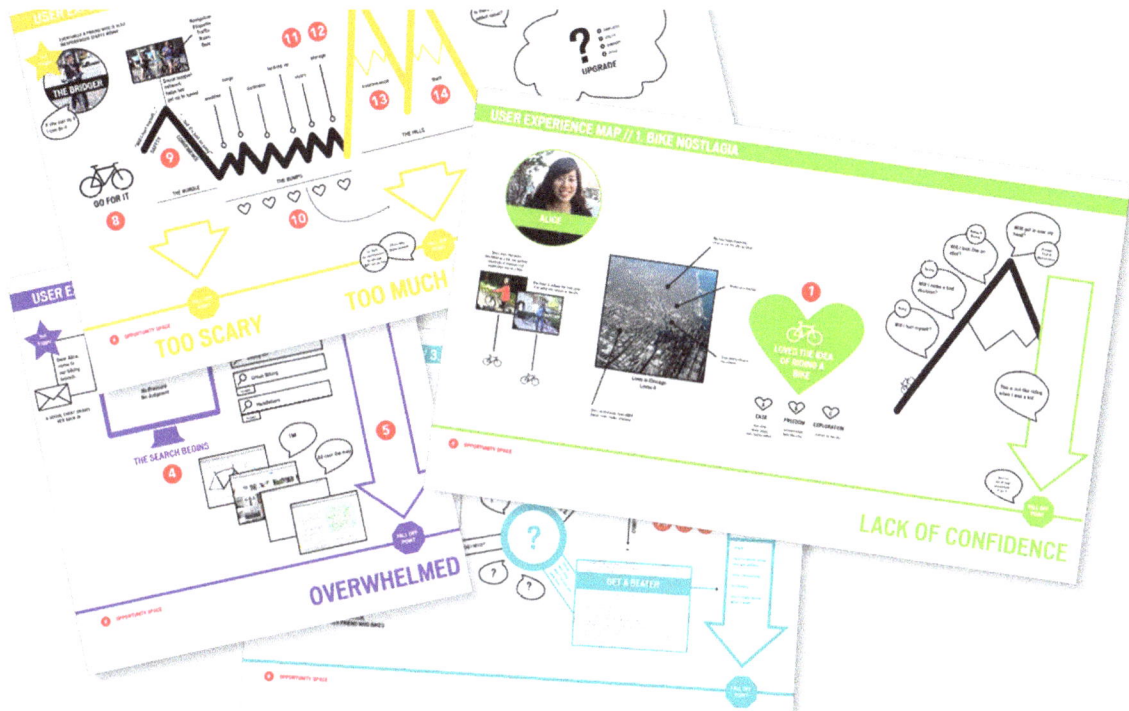

Source: Jamie Munger. Photo courtesy of Emergent Design.

Figure 10: Early Hunches

What gets in the way of a productive work day on the farm? How can we make a day of hard work easier in ways that count? To understand the daily challenges of workers, we drew up 30 sacrificial concepts (like the tool-finding application pictured here). We let farmers sort through the stack of concepts and tell us which ones represented real problems that needed solving and toss out those that do not. Then we asked them how they would improve the concepts for their own farm.

RFID = radio-frequency identification.

Source: Jamie Munger. Photo courtesy of Emergent Design.

Seeing through their eyes,
we learned that these
urbanites really love biking,
but not bikes.

▲ Visiting the homes of San Francisco residents to understand the realities of bike ownership in the city (photo courtesy of Emergent Design).

To come up with solutions for increasing bike riding in United States cities, my team combined several techniques to understand the variety of attitudes and experiences people have toward biking. Sensing that city riders are less concerned with premiere technologies and materials, we wanted to learn about what did matter to this group and what might convince them to get on a bike.

The team conducted **ethnographic interviews** with three different types of urbanites, each with a distinct mindset toward biking:

- ☐ **Skeptics.** People who are intrigued—but concerned—about city biking to understand perceived benefits and risks.
- ☐ **Newbies.** People who recently purchased their first bike to understand best practices for overcoming hurdles and concerns.
- ☐ **Lapsers.** People who recently stopped biking to understand why they quit.

Our research included in-home interviews, shop-alongs, and ride-alongs to gain a variety of perspectives on the benefits and pain points of city biking.

To learn about the associations people have with biking, we created a **cultural probe**: a game using cards and words, asking our participants to pull out three words that reminded them of biking and talk to us about each one. The most common ones were freedom, exploration, and independence.

We also had each participant create an **experience map** of their personal journey with biking. Many began their journeys in their childhood, reminiscing about happy memories of biking compared to more stressful adult biking experiences.

Seeing through their eyes, we learned that these urbanites really love biking—but not bikes. Biking is about freedom and urban exploration, but bikes themselves add complication, fear, and hassle. To get more people biking, we designed a bike membership service that eliminates negative aspects of biking while maximizing the freedom, exploration, and independence.

SYNTHESIS

Analyzing Findings into Actionable Insights

After research, the team has amassed a lot of information about end-users. The next step is to analyze these observations into actionable learnings. The goal is to identify insights and avoid the temptation of jumping too fast into solutions, thereby ignoring important themes. Synthesis requires "abstraction," a process through which observations from field research level up into overarching learnings. It sounds mysterious, but human-centered design has best practices and tools for facilitating this process.

- Visualize the team's collective thought process

- Cluster observations to reveal common themes

- Use flexible materials to freely explore connections

- Focus on insights, save solutions for later in a designated "parking lot" area

Redefining the Problem

Reframing the problem during synthesis is common practice and a positive sign. The team has seen the challenge from a new angle, pointing them toward more effective solutions.

Policy makers are accustomed to a more linear process, starting with a question and ending with an answer. Human-centered design uses an iterative process: each new cycle builds off insights from the previous cycle. It is expected that after each iteration, the definition of the problem needing to be solved has shifted. Reframes, while a natural part of the process, can feel like starting over if stakeholders are not prepared ahead of time.

All projects need a starting point. They set expectations about the problem to solve, why it matters, and what success looks like. Documents like the "terms of reference" inspire and focus the team so they can launch enthusiastically and effectively. But this brief is just a starting point; after research with beneficiaries the team will see the problem in a new light.

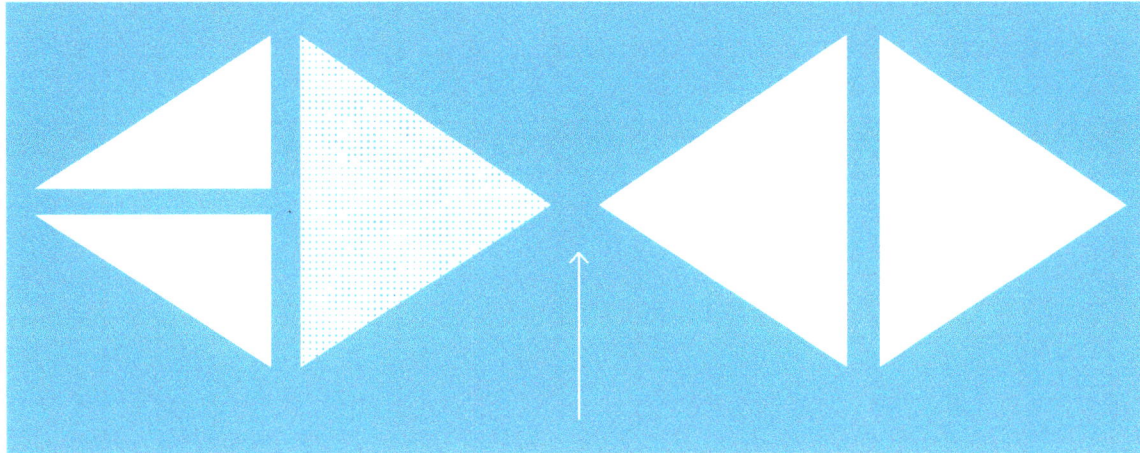

Figure 11: The Synthesis Phase

The synthesis phase is about defining the meaningful opportunities for change.

Source: Jamie Munger.

One example is a health-care organization that began with the question, "How might we develop new tools to help people more effectively quit smoking?" After learning that cutting down was in fact the best way for people to quit smoking, the problem was reframed to: "How might we make cutting down the natural on-ramp to quitting?" Being open to reframes allows for unexpected discoveries and more effective solutions.

Thematic Clustering

Through discussion of the field research, recurring topics and themes will emerge from the data. Creating clusters is a visual method for a team to identify patterns. This is a chance to revisit early hypotheses from contextual research and compare them to learnings from end-users.

Behavioral Frameworks

As themes emerge, the relationships between them are developed into behavioral frameworks. These visual representations can show, at a glance, how the users are affected by systems and issues. Frameworks are useful because they surface otherwise invisible relationships, and explain how and why people are affected by them.

Personas

Personas (sometimes called typologies) are profiles of different types of users based on their attitudes, experiences, and motivations. Personas are not the same as market segmentations, which are predominantly drawn from demographic factors like age, location, income, or gender. These human portraits reflect insights, themes, and patterns to illustrate key differences between user groups. They are useful for identifying common problems that need to be solved in different ways for different users, and also for selecting the best target users moving forward.

Opportunity Areas

The last step in synthesis is to translate insights into opportunities. Opportunity areas are a bridge to move from thinking about the current state, toward envisioning how things could be better in the future. They are often phrased as thought-provoking questions beginning with the words "how might we . . . ?" Opportunity areas are used to spark idea generation, but are not ideas themselves. Be cautious of opportunity areas that only point to one type of solution, as they should suggest many possibilities instead of just one. An opportunity area is a rearticulation of user needs that is future facing, optimistic, and inspiring.

Figure 12: Entrepreneurship Journey

What is the experience of starting a start-up at the University of Chicago? What influences whether they succeed or fail? A very confusing journey is visualized here. The journey has many fall-off points and very few launching-off points. This framework helped define the areas entrepreneurs need support to keep their momentum going.

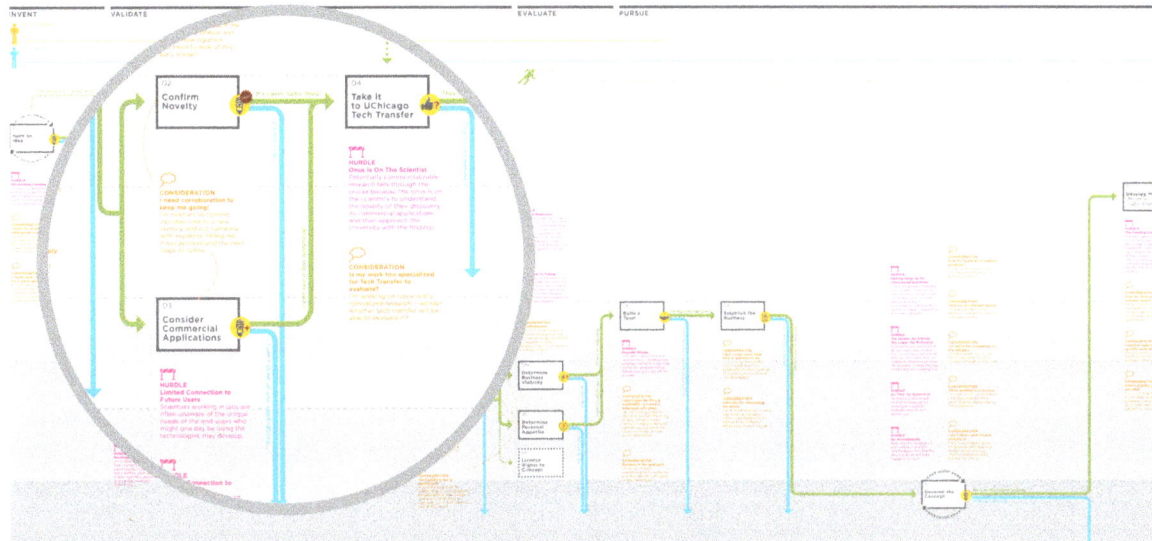

Source: Photo courtesy of Emergent Design.

Figure 13: Maintaining Momentum

The University of Chicago momentum framework became the strategic foundation for services and programs to foster innovation at the university. Immersive research with student and faculty entrepreneurs revealed that to maintain their momentum, these three overlapping needs must be met: process clarity, career promise, and concept growth.

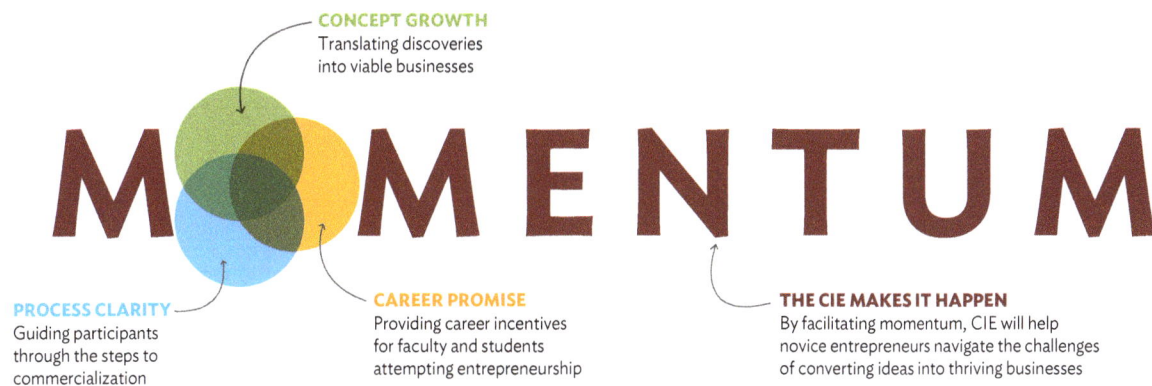

CONCEPT GROWTH
Translating discoveries into viable businesses

PROCESS CLARITY
Guiding participants through the steps to commercialization

CAREER PROMISE
Providing career incentives for faculty and students attempting entrepreneurship

THE CIE MAKES IT HAPPEN
By facilitating momentum, CIE will help novice entrepreneurs navigate the challenges of converting ideas into thriving businesses

CIE = Chicago Innovation Exchange.
Source: Photo courtesy of Emergent Design.

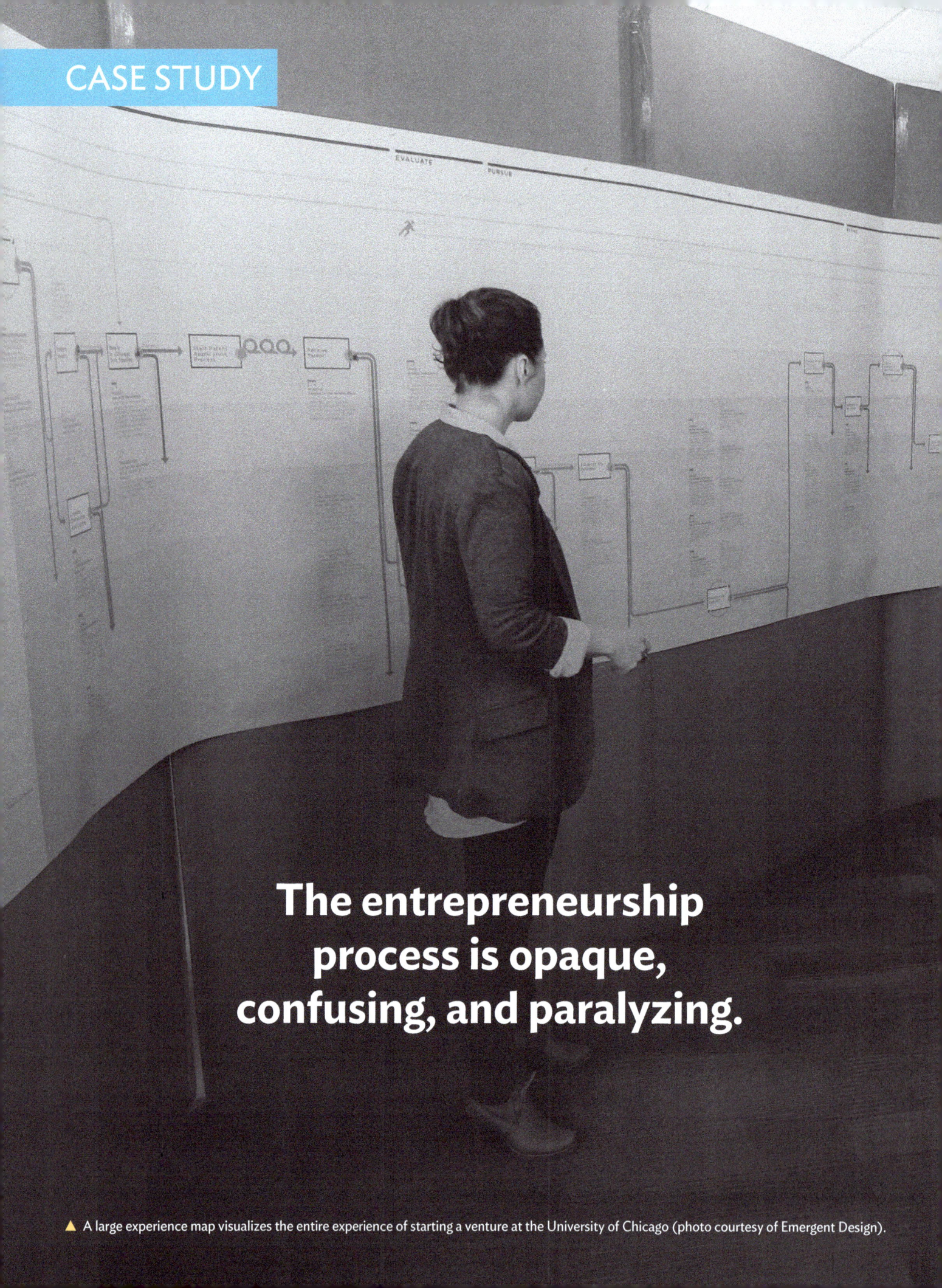

The entrepreneurship process is opaque, confusing, and paralyzing.

▲ A large experience map visualizes the entire experience of starting a venture at the University of Chicago (photo courtesy of Emergent Design).

The University of Chicago set forth a new policy to increase entrepreneurship and innovation at the university. The first investment was building a multimillion dollar high-technology innovation center. To understand what programs and services should be offered inside the building, my team spent several months interviewing and shadowing faculty and students to understand their experiences with entrepreneurship, and how it matched up with their professional motivations, aspirations, and limitations.

Not surprisingly at a premiere research institution like the University of Chicago, the faculty was deeply motivated by learning and intellectual stimulation. This would seemingly make them enthusiastic to take on new challenges, like entrepreneurship. We found three areas where this enthusiasm was accidentally stifled by conflicting academic policies:

☐ **Career promise.** Participation in entrepreneurship activities did not support the tenure track, making it professionally risky.

☐ **Process clarity.** The entrepreneurship process is opaque, confusing, and paralyzing, making it easy to lose momentum.

☐ **Concept growth.** Entrepreneurs had no tools for assessing their own progress, making it difficult to evaluate their own success.

By bringing these pain points to the surface, my team was able to introduce a new framework for fostering innovation at the university. Deans and department heads used these findings to develop professional incentives, and my team developed a tool to make the process more straightforward. We saw three significant opportunities to eliminate confusion and empower entrepreneurs: seeing the big picture, knowing next steps, and connecting to resources.

To develop these opportunities into programs and services, we created **low-fidelity prototypes**. Using large posters and smaller pieces of paper, we made an interactive diagram of the process of entrepreneurship and the corresponding activities, resources, and outcomes at each step. Then we took this prototype to different experts and end-users to get their feedback. The end result was a guidebook called *The Innovation Pathway*.[a] It is a practical tool designed to help academic start-ups maintain their momentum. The book is currently used to vet, recruit, and bring on aspiring entrepreneurs at the University of Chicago.

[a] J. Munger and W. Skelton. 2014. *The Innovation Pathway*. Chicago: University of Chicago.

PROTOTYPING

Exploring Many Possible Solutions Until the Best Set Is Defined

Human-centered designers look to end-users for feedback on new ideas by creating quick and inexpensive prototypes to explore many possible solutions. The goal is to learn from these reactions and refine the solutions before substantial investment. At first, prototyping is a way to ask and answer questions about new ideas. Are they valuable? Do they solve the right problems? Do they make sense? As concepts become more refined, the prototypes help define preferences for usability and aesthetics.

- Uncover big problems early on
- Get feedback on the idea, separately from the aesthetics
- Avoid falling in love with wrong idea
- Refine ideas cheaply and quickly

Refining Solutions and Preparing to Launch

After the prototyping phase, the new products, services, and programs are ready for pilot, final refinement, and launch. The bulk of detailed planning happens during the implementation phase. This often requires bringing in different types of experts to flesh out the specifics—engineers, partner organizations, operations specialists, and funders.

Organizations often prefer to use their own teams and partners for implementation. The human-centered design team starts to hand off their work through workshops and trainings, so the implementing teams can take over.

Figure 14: The Prototyping Phase

The prototyping phase is about refining solutions by getting feedback from beneficiaries.

Source: Jamie Munger.

Shifting Focus from Policy to Experience

People do not experience policy: people have experiences. Experiences are how any type of offering—be it a product, policy, program, or technology—comes to life. Experiences are important because they are memorable; they stick. Beneficiaries relive positive ones and remember to avoid negative ones.

When organizations focus only on their core offering, without understanding the overall experience it is a part of, they risk creating experiences that stick for the wrong reasons. Prototyping different ways a policy can play out from the beneficiary perspective helps ensure that the intent is reflected in the services that bring it to life.

Scenario Maps

Experiences, in their entirety, are difficult to see. Design thinkers use scenario maps to visualize multifaceted experiences through the eyes of the end-user. It is a way to explore the interplay between motivations, priorities, options, and activities to design an experience that is memorable for the right reasons.

Provotypes

A provotype is a physical representation of a thought-provoking, open-ended question. It is an object, or an interaction, that provokes reactions the researchers can learn from. Unlike a prototype, it does not suggest an answer. It is usually introduced early in the design process as a means to simulate conversation about the future.

Low-Fidelity Prototypes

Low-fidelity prototypes are used to narrow down and refine new ideas by getting feedback from end-users. The term "low fidelity" means that the aesthetics are basic and materials are inexpensive; the prototypes are quick, cheap, and easy to produce. The priority for low-fidelity prototypes is to convey the conceptual center of new ideas then invite candid feedback. Even teams with large budgets use low-fidelity prototypes because this technique is most effective for eliciting user input on the idea itself without getting distracted by secondary details, like aesthetics.

Through prototyping and iteration, solutions become more refined and prototypes gain higher fidelity. High fidelity prototypes are used for refining aesthetics, testing usability, and validating uptake.

Experience Prototypes

Experience prototypes are used to develop services and programs that unfold over a longer period of time. Experience prototypes involve choosing key moments of a new service concept and finding a way to represent them to get feedback from end-users. To begin, something as simple as a storyboard can work. It is not necessary to prototype every aspect of a service at the same time. Testing out different elements of the service separately is a way to keep refining the concepts without investing in a pilot too early.

Exploring New Ideas

To get feedback on a variety of physical and digital product ideas for smoking cessation, we developed 22 low-fidelity prototypes out of paper and store-bought materials. Putting them in the hands of people trying to quit helped us explore different options and refine the best ones.

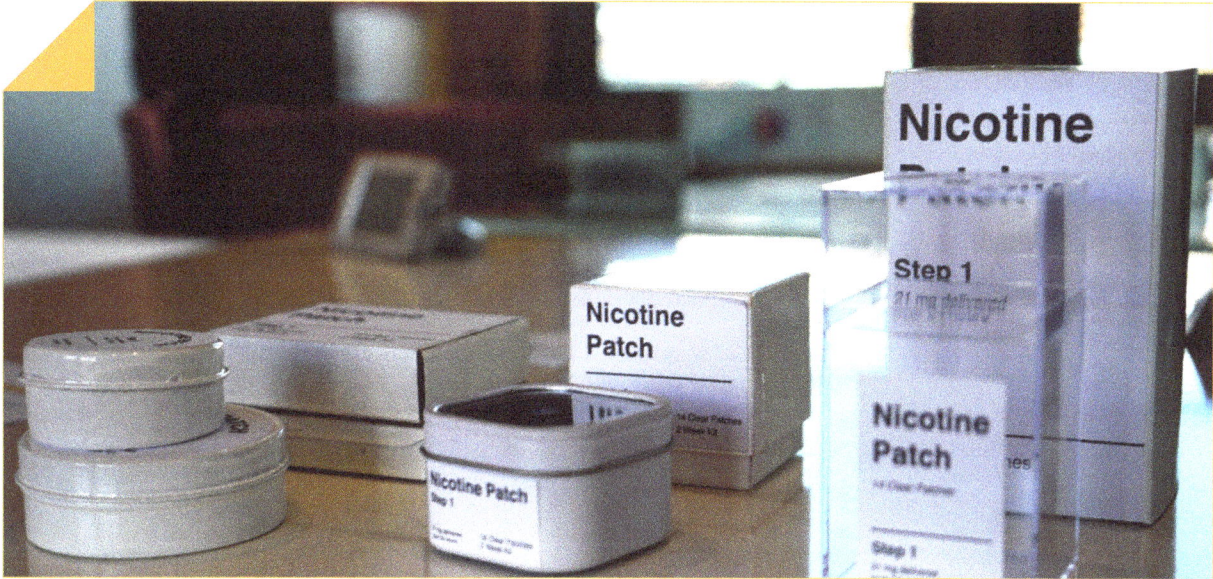

Source: Photo courtesy of Emergent Design.

Prototyping a Service

To figure out which features of a new bike service were the most compelling to riders, we made a service prototype using a local bike tour group, 25 bikes, one big red van, large bright posters, and pocket-sized pamphlets.
We hosted four groups of riders on a tour, observed their reactions, and asked for their feedback.
By the end, we knew which aspects of the service were compelling and which ones we could eliminate.

Source: Photo courtesy of Emergent Design.

Would they take time away from their work to give it a shot?

▲ Farmer in Boyer, Haiti attending an educational program at the local school (photo courtesy of Emergent Design).

A few years ago, my team was on a project in a remote part of Haiti's central plateau. Here was a community of farmers who urgently needed infrastructure to water their crops. Though the farms were beside a large river, without pipes and pumps there was no way to transport enough water to the crops during a drought. The time frame for funding, planning, digging, and building the pipes was around 2 years. An alternative short-term fix was needed.

The need for water infrastructure was urgent, but there was no way for my client, a tuition-free elementary school, to solve it with their capabilities and resources. We needed to find a solution that was **viable, desirable, and feasible** or nothing would happen at all.

Through immersive research with the farming community, we found three individuals who had managed to keep their crops going, despite the drought. Spending time with them, we learned some simple things they were doing differently from their neighbors. Sharing these simple techniques through a free agricultural program had the power to make a huge difference for the community. Most importantly, the program fit the resources and capabilities the school had to offer.

Designing the agriculture education program for farmers raised important questions about whether people would attend. Would they take time away from their work to give it a shot?

To answer these questions, we developed a **provotype**. We hired an entrepreneurship lecturer to give a free, 1-day seminar for anyone wanting to attend. Two days beforehand, we sent the students home with letters to their parents, explaining the event and inviting them to join. At 2 p.m., only a handful of people were there, and we wondered if our agriculture education program was going to work. By 3 p.m., almost 200 people showed up, proving to us that the farmers were indeed interested and willing to take time away from their busy farm work for an education program.

This provotype gave us the confidence to keep going with the curriculum design, knowing that there was desire for the program from the community.

CHAPTER 4

CASE STUDY

This chapter is devoted to a single project
from the Government of Indonesia
and the Asian Development Bank
to look at the true impacts
of educational policies on seafarers.

MARITIME EDUCATION

In 2017, Indonesia launched an exploratory project to better understand the real human impact of their maritime education and training (MET) system. MET is a vocational nationwide system that educates students to become seafarers: crew, engineers, and officers working on commercial ships. For Indonesia, the commercial shipping sector holds great promise. The country has 81,000 kilometers of coastline and a prime location along three of the world's biggest maritime highways.

Unfortunately, data indicated that something was off with the maritime education system.[9] Vast numbers of graduates were unable to pass their exams. Those that did pass still waited 6 months to 1 year to find a job. Meanwhile, employers reported an abundance of semi-skilled workers, but too few were highly skilled.

A misalignment between the international commercial shipping industry and Indonesia's educational system threatened the success of Indonesia's sizable investments in modernizing the maritime sector.

At the request of the Government of Indonesia, the Asian Development Bank (ADB) commissioned an exploratory study to look at the MET from three perspectives: industry, education, and people. The maritime study combined traditional quantitative methodologies with a new approach—human-centered design—to show how policies affected beneficiaries.[10]

---

[9] Maritime education, training, and certification is regulated internationally by the International Maritime Organization (IMO), a United Nations special agency, and seafarers must meet IMO certification requirements for each task performed and for each rank held. MET systems are accredited at the country level and loss of accreditation has dire consequences for seafarers as all past and present certificates issued by that country are invalidated.

[10] Education Sector Analytical and Capacity Development Partnership (ACDP-026). 2017. *Preparing Skilled and Highly Skilled Manpower for Indonesia's Modernizing Maritime Sector.* Jakarta: ACDP.

▲ Vocational high school students in Saparua, Indonesia.
Source: Education Sector Analytical and Capacity Development Partnership (ACDP-026). 2017. *Preparing Skilled and Highly Skilled Manpower for Indonesia's Modernizing Maritime Sector. Human-centered Design Case Study. Analysis of Seafarer Pathways to Certification and Employment.* Jakarta: ACDP (reprinted with permission).

Project Goals

The goal of this work was to use a new methodology—human-centered design—along with traditional research approaches—economic and educational policy analysis—to create a holistic assessment of the maritime education system and the people it is intended to serve.

- Use a new methodology
- Understand how the system affects people
- Combine human, economic, and educational insights

The Maritime Sector

Ninety percent of the world's goods are transported by sea. Food, industrial materials, electronics, medicines, even animals, move from one country to the next on ships. Countries located along the deep international sea lanes along which these goods must travel are strategically positioned to benefit. Indonesia is one of these countries, with 81,000 kilometers of coastline and a prime location along three of the world's biggest maritime highways. Forty percent of commercial sea traffic passes through oceans in and around Indonesia; unfortunately all but about 10% of that traffic literally passes by Indonesia. The president, Joko Widodo, intended to change that by modernizing the sector, thereby transforming the country into a world-class maritime axis.

A HOLISTIC APPROACH

The maritime study looked separately at three perspectives—those of industry, education, and seafarers—to understand the true nature of how policies affect the students and their careers as seafarers. Like any industry, the success of the maritime sector depends heavily on the education system. The schools play dual roles: (i) to provide labor for the growing industry's needs; and (ii) to provide students with options for a better, more fulfilling life. The sector and the people within it evaluate success quite differently. Success to people is usually qualitative, while industry and education measure impact quantitatively. The goal was for all types of success to align. Therefore, a holistic approach was needed.

The Industry Perspective

The shipping industry depends on formal vocational schools offering programs at the senior secondary and higher education levels as well as informal training through short courses to prepare the right quantity and quality of seafarers. How many seafarers are needed? How many officers and how many ratings? The goal of the industry perspective was to define the "right size" of the system using economic analysis of supply and demand. Data indicated that these forces were misaligned; there were too many semi-skilled seafarers and not enough skilled seafarers coming out of the schools.

In the end, data around the industry perspective was conflicted. Some sources reported an immediate need for tens of thousands of new seafarers. Other sources claimed an oversupply of lower-skilled workers, but a sufficient supply of higher-skilled workers to meet the present demand. Most sources agree on one thing: the problem is not with the quantity of seafarers, but with the quality of their education and training.

The Education Perspective

An analysis of the Indonesian MET system revealed policy-level contradictions. The International Maritime Organization (IMO) accredits Indonesia's MET system under Indonesian law.

The Ministry of Transportation sets the standards for MET providers, assessors, seafarers' competency, and proficiency levels in accordance with the international agreement on the Standards of Training Certification and Watchkeeping Code. At the same time, by Indonesian law, all education providers offering diplomas or degrees must be accredited using standards set forth in the Education Law and the Higher Education Law.

These statutes are nearly impossible to reconcile. As a result, as of 2016, only 3 out of 178 accredited vocational secondary schools offering MET programs were approved by the Ministry of Transportation and only 11 out of 25 accredited higher education institutions met minimum standards for Ministry of Transportation approval. As IMO guidelines stipulate, only graduates from approved METs can take the examination for certification upon graduation; most graduates from unapproved programs must go through a long and expensive process to obtain certification that can take 3 years or more to complete.

MET is not unique. Many vocational programs would benefit from a less rigid education framework. A more flexible framework would empower MET to provide quality programs for their students, while also responding to modernizing industry needs.

The Seafarer Perspective

Using human-centered design to understand the true impact MET policy on students and seafarers revealed that beneficiaries were caught up in a dysfunctional system. There were six unofficial career pathways a student could take to become a seafarer. Interviews with 58 seafarers and students revealed they were often held back by the system intended to support them. Bureaucratic entanglement, lack of transparency, and process inconsistencies caused them uncertainty and confusion, and stymied their ability to make informed decisions.

Challenges were not just at the front end of education but also at mid-career. To advance professionally, seafarers were required to take additional courses. The confusion and uncertainty that typified their early schooling continued throughout their career. The sections that follow will dive into their experiences with MET during three crucial career phases: choosing their career, sea service, and mid-career growth.

PROCESS

Context

To prepare for research with students and seafarers, a baseline understanding of the current state of maritime education came from discussions with experts and beginners. The human-centered design team used two techniques previously discussed in the context chapter, expert interviews, and social listening (p. 31). The expert and beginner perspectives led to early hypotheses and hunches that would be explored more deeply during in-person interviews.

Expert interviews with Indonesia's education specialists provided insight on the challenges already known to affect MET quality. For example, many teachers struggled to prepare the next generation of seafarers for highly technical careers at sea because they never gained work experience themselves on real ships. Seafaring is a highly technical field; classroom simulations are not a substitute for hands-on experience. Low-quality teachers were both a symptom and a cause of the dysfunctional system.

Understanding the experience of beginners, through social listening, provided insight on what it is really like to be a prospective student. Observing conversations taking place on public internet forums, such as Facebook, Twitter, job boards, and YouTube, revealed a chaotic and confusing scene. Credible sources were indistinguishable from deceptive ones, making it impossible to know what information to trust. Patterns, pain points, and hypotheses gleaned from the expert and beginning perspectives prepared the team for in-depth conversations with students and seafarers themselves.

Research

The research involved field studies and ethnographic interviews with 58 individual students and seafarers across five different cities. Each interview included hands-on activities to dive into key themes identified during the context phase.

Career Pathways

What is the experience of becoming a seafarer? What are the steps, resources, and fall-off points? Experiences, in their entirety, are difficult to see. The team used experience maps to visualize the different pathways students take through MET. Each person drew their own career journey in their own words, paying special attention to the highs and lows.

BPN = Balikpapan (Kalimantan), JKT = Jakarta.

Source: Education Sector Analytical and Capacity Development Partnership (ACDP-026). 2017. *Preparing Skilled and Highly Skilled Manpower for Indonesia's Modernizing Maritime Sector.* Jakarta: ACDP.

Indah JKT   Sunarno JKT   Bambang JKT

Surjadi JKT   Karno BPN   Tedi BPN

Jhoni BPN   Niko BPN   Iwan BPN

Trusted Information

How do students find information? What sources do they trust? The team used cultural probes to understand trust from the student perspective. Each student created a map of their information sources and ranked them from most trusted to least. The probe revealed that the most trusted sources of information were always people, while the least trusted were institutions. Students looked to friends, peers, alumni, and family, yet did not have a way of determining if their information was accurate.

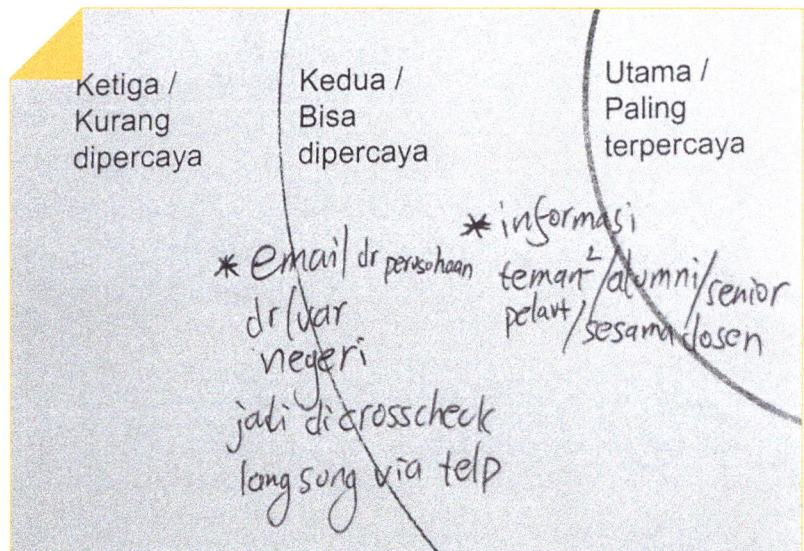

Ketiga / Kurang dipercaya   Kedua / Bisa dipercaya   Utama / Paling terpercaya

Source: Education Sector Analytical and Capacity Development Partnership (ACDP-026). 2017. *Preparing Skilled and Highly Skilled Manpower for Indonesia's Modernizing Maritime Sector.* Jakarta: ACDP.

Synthesis

After the research was complete, the human-centered design team looked for themes and patterns within the 58 multifaceted experiences of students and seafarers. They identified six personas, each with a different career pathway and a different experience with MET.

The personas were composite portraits, based on themes and patterns observed in real people and representing the diverse group of students, seafarers, teachers, and employers who used, or might use, the MET system. They were helpful for stakeholders who did not have daily interactions with people in the maritime industry, yet were responsible for creating processes, programs, services, and protocols that directly affect these people's lives.

Looking at the career pathway for each persona reveals that beneficiaries tended to struggle with during the same three phases: choosing their career, sea service, and mid-career growth. The pathways highlight key interactions with MET that hampered, confused, and disappointed, due to poor communication or conflicting frameworks at the system level.

Once these pain points were named, the career pathways were used to define how the beneficiaries' experiences could be improved, and then to align MET stakeholders around that vision. Along each journey were ideas for new programs or interventions that could prevent drop out at low points.

Prior to this work, stakeholders in the maritime education system did not have a nuanced portrait of the different beneficiaries and their career experiences. Building personas, journey maps, and concepts was the starting point for aligning policy initiatives with the people at the heart of the education system.

Seafarer Personas

Six different personas function as stand-ins for MET-system-users' needs, attitudes, and motivations.

The Go-Getter Seafarers

"I want to get ANT I before turning 40."

- Goal-oriented (purposeful)
- Smart and resourceful
- Take initiative
- Consistent, good attitude
- Optimistic
- Ready to leave (their hometown) but keen to share back to their community

The Feminist Seafarers

"I love my family, but I love the sea more."

- Passionate about being at sea
- Equal Work Opportunity activists, often as a result of unfair rejection from employers
- High drive to prove their competency
- High sense of responsibility to nurture young female seafarers
- This persona may not necessarily apply to all women seafarers

The Uninformed-yet-Strong-willed Seafarers

"I just bought a ticket and off I go … guess it'll be reimbursed later?"

- Lack of initiative to look for available resources
- Confused because of limited information and network
- Hardworking but lack of strategic thinking
- Act on impulse because of desperation (do whatever it takes!)
- Follow what others say should be the right thing to do
- Turn pessimistic/bitter over time

The Stepping-Stone Seafarers

"I was told this is a good path, but it'll be a temporary thing for me."

- Pursuing maritime mostly for its financial promise, as a stepping-stone to higher earnings in their actual dream job
- Practical and pragmatic in making decisions
- Not their real "dream"
- Already plan to be back on land during school time
- May become pessimistic from witnessing what they call "monkey business" within the industry

The Happy-Go-Lucky Seafarers

"I accidentally stepped into this … so far so good!"

- Go with the "flow"
- Stumbled upon maritime unintentionally
- Pursued formal/academic education
- Positive mindset, grounded optimist
- Got the right opportunity by being in the right place, with the right attitude, at the right time
- Content with their career progress, plan to leave legacy by passing on knowledge and stories

The Unplanned Seafarers

"I was given the chance, so I took it and hope for the best."

- Not formally educated, low academic foundation
- Got into the job by chance
- Aspire to climb the rank ladder, understand own limitation but helpless
- Good attitude at work
- Work atmosphere matters (peers that are kind to them)
- Not many career options (mostly labor intensive)

Note: ANT I refers to the certification required to become captain.

Source: Education Sector Analytical and Capacity Development Partnership (ACDP-026). 2017. *Preparing Skilled and Highly Skilled Manpower for Indonesia's Modernizing Maritime Sector.* Jakarta: ACDP.

Journey Maps

The journey maps revealed pain points in the current experience, and ideas for how to address them in the future.

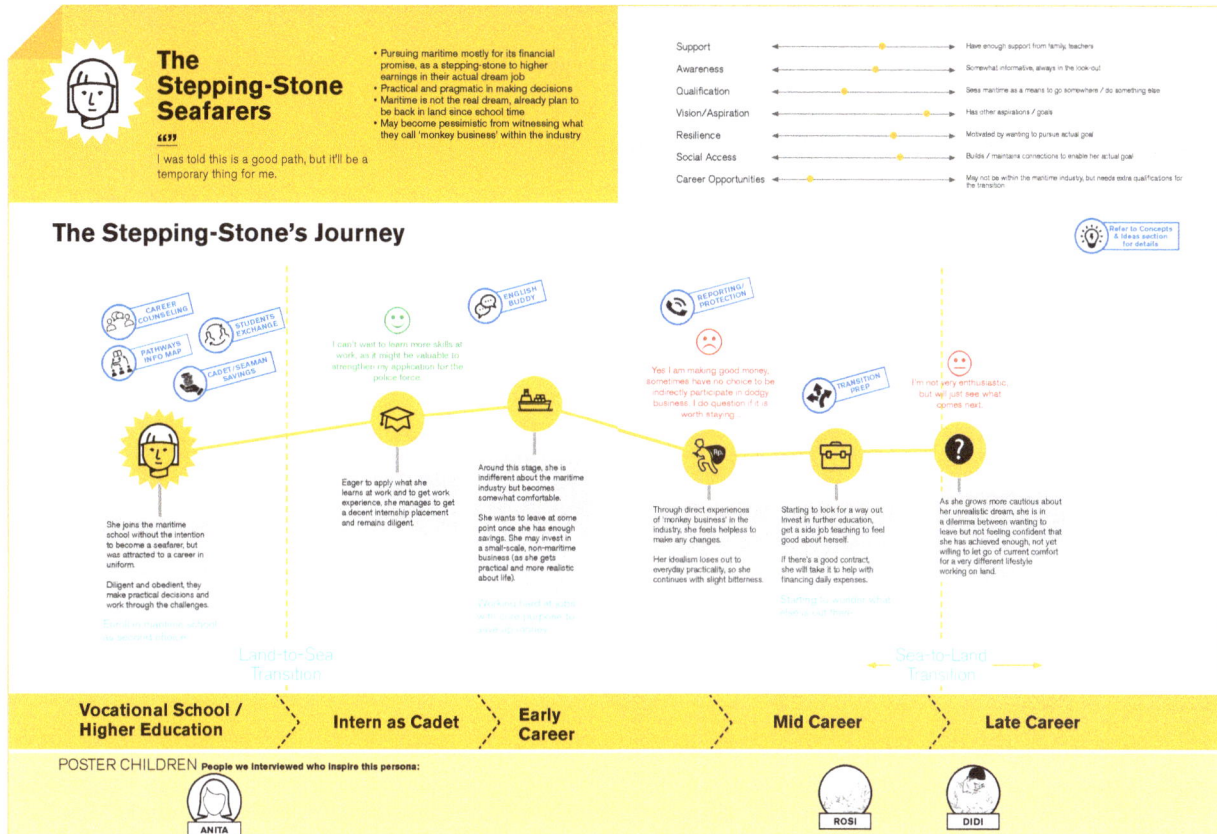

Source: Education Sector Analytical and Capacity Development Partnership (ACDP-026). 2017. *Preparing Skilled and Highly Skilled Manpower for Indonesia's Modernizing Maritime Sector.* Jakarta: ACDP.

CHOOSING A CAREER

This section will focus on key findings from the interviews with students and seafarers. It is organized around three crucial phases: choosing their career, sea service, and mid-career growth.

The Promise Is Not the Reality

❝ Even somebody like me can go and see the world, so anyone can. ❞

—Wellem, seafarer

The seafarer profession has cache; it implies both economic and social status. The uniform is a symbol of discipline and leadership. Life at sea offers an opportunity to travel the world. The career carries an expectation of upward mobility. In reality, seafarers fall into two categories: ratings and officers. The officers are highly skilled, rigorously trained, and well paid. The ratings have less training and less pay.

Young men and women can choose a maritime career as early as 15, when they start secondary school. Across Indonesia, 178 secondary schools offer a vocational education in maritime studies. Others might decide at age 18 to attend one of the 25 higher education institutions. Choosing to attend any of these schools is often a family investment because of the tuition and other fees associated with both public and private schools.

Cadets are often bewildered upon graduation to find they are not prepared by their education to meet the licensing requirements to apply for work. They do not get support from their school to understand what to do next. What follows are several years of trying to obtain the necessary training to get their first job on a ship at their own expense. Without an accurate, centralized source of information to guide them, the pathway toward that first job is often confusing, expensive, and time-consuming.

Most Indonesian Schools Do Not Meet International Standards

❝ In this maritime world, we can only depend on ourselves. ❞

—Wawan, seafarer

Cadets experience an education that does not meet the international standards for maritime training. Most of the secondary level curriculum is not relevant to their career. Their teachers range in qualification, and many have no sea experience at all. Only 3 out of the 178 secondary schools meet the international standards and only 11 out of 25 higher education schools meet the international standards.

Would-be students have to choose from a huge diversity of schools, without guidance on how to choose. There is no standard for maritime curriculum, teacher qualification, facility, or quality assurance. The schools get to decide what standards they are capable of meeting. Lucky and/or well-informed students wind up in one of the schools that meets international standards.

Reliable Information Is Hard to Come By

Without an accurate centralized source of information to guide them, cadets must find their own way. They depend heavily on one another for information. Applicants learn about careers and study programs primarily through stories shared by teachers, relatives, or friends. The informers are likely to be uninformed themselves, and the information is likely to be inaccurate, unreliable, or biased. Applicants are often confused about careers, program costs, duration, graduation requirements, and post-graduation certification requirement.

Unforeseen Certification Costs
Drive Students into Debt

❝ He had spent all of his money; some of us who had passed the exam raised some money for him to take another exam. **❞**

—Eksan, cadet

Understanding the certifications needed to get a license is often unclear, and students and their families are not able to find the proper information to prepare. In particular, they have no idea how much it will cost.

Many students are confused about what maritime jobs actually entail, and the types of certifications needed. For example, working on a tanker and working on a cruise ship require different certificates. It is particularly confusing for young cadets. Clear and accurate descriptions of the options, including how and where to obtain certificates, is difficult to find.

Cadets must save up, or have solid financing plans, to afford the certifications that lead to jobs on ships. Yet, many prospective students enter maritime school unaware of the costs involved. While some schools help manage students' expectations, others mislead applicants. Most families find that the cost and length of schooling is much greater than they were told.

Some Cadets Will Cheat the System,
Because It Has Cheated Them

Some cadets falsify or lie about their credentials to get a job. This makes employers suspicious of Indonesian seafarers, and stokes the perception that they are not well trained and not trustworthy. The industry's response to this fraud is to develop their own exams, further fragmenting an already chaotic system.

SEA SERVICE

A Career Defining Stepping-Stone

" It is important that during their internship the cadets really learn about their future job, so that they can walk out and feel ready to do his or her job. "

—Jhoni, ship captain

Once students have completed their maritime studies, they are anxious to complete their credentials and exams so they can begin work. A critical stepping-stone is the required internship at sea, or "sea service." Sea service is required for cadets to get their first job. It can take between 1 and 3 years, depending on what position they are training for.

Sea service is a major differentiator for students' success once they are in the job market. Those who performed well during their internship might be offered a contract with the company after graduation. Cadets learn crucial skills that employers will look for—English, comfort with certain machinery, an understanding of international maritime laws, and leadership skills. Not all sea service internships offer the same quality of experience for the cadets.

Essential Yet Absent from Most Programs

Students at most schools find that sea service is not part of the curriculum. Graduates must take an additional program that takes at least 3 more years, and more money, to complete. Instead of the year-long sea service, some secondary schools offer 2-week to 3-month sea-based internships. These internships do not meet the international standards for 1 year of sea training prior to taking examinations. Often, these internships entail serving food and performing chores that are unrelated to technical knowledge that qualifies them for a job.

Waiting for Sea Service Placement Comes at a High Cost

“ Sometimes we teachers have to beg the companies to accept the students to do whatever work is available on the ships. **”**

—Trisha, teacher

There is a severe bottleneck at the sea service stage. Cadets applying to get a placement can wait as long as a year or more. This idle time is expensive because that they cannot use it to further their career. Many take other jobs or drop out. Others give up on being an officer and decide to become a lower paid rating during this time.

The Burden Is Transferred to Students and Teachers

“ We are exhausted from looking for companies. Each of them only take one to two students. Where will the other twenty go? **”**

—Lisa, teacher

The burden falls on students to figure out sea service for themselves, and also on teachers to try and find good opportunities for their students.

MID-CAREER GROWTH

Moving Up, Then Moving Out

❝ My move to sail abroad has its risks, far away from family. If I just work on the local ferry, life will just stay this way, not much improvements. Yes, the cost for the school is expensive, but actually it is not a matter of school fees, but the cost of living during courses. So I want to make one step but [that] has big impact. ❞

—Arnold, aspiring ship captain

The appeal of a career at sea is the ability to move up professionally, financially, and socially. Seafarers begin as ratings, or low-level officers, and then hope to move up the ladder over time. In reality, many cannot find their first job, there is no opportunity to move up, or they get stuck in low-level positions without the resources for certifications required to move up.

To progress professionally, seafarers must get more education to obtain specific certifications. Each new level requires courses, certifications, and sea service. Additional training makes it possible to move up the chain of command into the higher-skilled and higher-paying positions, or to seek out careers on land.

Growth Requires Knowledge, Planning, and Resources

Many officers want to move up the chain of command to earn more responsibility and higher-paid positions. This requires a solid grasp of the career options and a financial plan for achieving them. Certification at each level is expensive and financing is an important consideration, resulting in career stagnation at the junior officer level. In 2016, nearly 50% of certified officers, most of them junior level, were not working on vessels. There is a lot the officers do not know, which prevents them from planning effectively.

Officers are not always clear on what career options will not become obsolete, which certifications are needed, and how much time and financing they should plan for. For junior officers who wish to move up the career ladder, obtaining next-level certifications is often beyond their reach.

Inexperienced Seafarers Drag Down Education as Teachers

" How can they produce competent seafarers if the teachers themselves have minimal work experience? "

—Surjadi, crewing manager and
ex-captain of an international shipping line

Many teachers are junior officers who were unable to find employment at sea. This phenomenon perpetuates the poor training many cadets experience because the teachers cannot effectively train their students.

Key Takeaways

WHAT'S NEEDED ARE BETTER SCHOOLS, NOT MORE OF THEM

The number of maritime schools and programs in Indonesia is sufficient to meet the demands of the industry. What is needed is a higher-quality program to better prepare seafarers for their careers.

QUALITY DEPENDS ON RESOLVING THE CONTRADICTIONS BETWEEN MINISTRIES

The most effective way to improve MET quality is to align all ministries so that all programs are held to the same international standards. Based on this study, the involved ministries initiated this alignment.

EDUCATIONAL CHALLENGES ARE NOT JUST AT THE FRONT END, BUT ALSO AT MID-CAREER

The MET plays an important role in beneficiaries' careers well past graduation. Improving the system means also addressing the pain points that seafarers experience while climbing the career ladder.

POOR-QUALITY TEACHERS ARE A SYMPTOM AND CAUSE OF POOR-QUALITY EDUCATION

Breaking the cycle of poor-quality education means teachers need work experience to draw from.

CHAPTER 5

LESSONS LEARNED

Five practical insights
about the practice of
human-centered design
for policy makers.

FOR POLICY MAKERS

Increasing numbers of policy makers see the value of human-centered design (or design thinking) to help them find the overlap between what is viable, desirable, and feasible. The methodology can be powerful when used in combination with other inputs, such as economic analysis, big data, or specialist expertise, to guide decision-making and policy design. Human-centered design applied to policy is still new and case studies are few and far between.

To close this book, we provide six insights about the practice itself. These insights address common myths and misconceptions about design thinking and demonstrate how it adds value by helping policy makers get closer to beneficiaries, uncover their unmet needs, and develop innovative products and services to meet those needs.

Innovation Is Not Always about a Big Bang

Policy makers want to innovate—everyone does—but what exactly does that mean? Organizations often assume that innovation must require inventing something brand-new. More often, innovation is about finding new ways to apply existing ideas. Brand-new solutions take decades to come to market. Driverless cars were invented in the 1920s, working prototypes appeared in the 1980s, and regulation began permitting their use in the 2010s. Policy makers cannot wait 100 years to make an impact.

Most innovation is about combining best practices from diverse sources, and trailblazing around the details. Design thinking has become synonymous with innovation partly because it is uniquely capable of surfacing best practices. Field research brings researchers into close contact with people's personal, professional, and social lives. Here, they learn the techniques people develop for solving their own challenges in simple, clever, and economical ways. These best practices can be modified and combined to develop innovative solutions at scale.

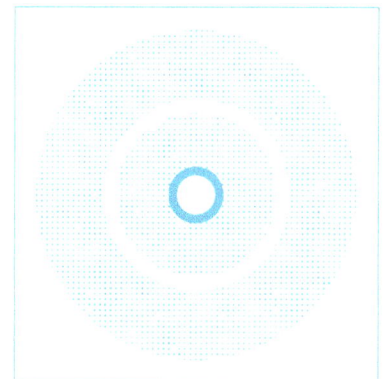

Organizations sometimes feel the need to be creative in big ways, when in fact what is needed is a new application of something that has already proven to work.

Innovation Is Not the Same as Technology

Organizations looking for innovation often assume the answer must lie in technology. Without understanding how technologies are experienced and received by beneficiaries, enormous investments can go to waste, resulting in empty computer labs, untouched state-of-the-art lab equipment, and lifesaving medical devices left in the box.

Technology can bedazzle decision makers with its capabilities, without considering the human context in which it will operate. While a technology might be able to accomplish some tasks more efficiently, it might also ask something unacceptable of the person who is supposed to use it. Technology solves some problems, leaves others untouched, and often creates new ones. The result can be rejection of the technology outright.

Take the example of home monitoring systems. In theory, these systems provide caretakers with peace of mind by detecting when their older parents or loved ones have a medical emergency at home. In reality, older adults reject this potentially lifesaving technology because it feels infantilizing and obtrusive.

Technology is not innovation if it does not pay attention to the real human experience. Design thinking first understands the problem by considering people and their cultural, physical, and psychological contexts, then solves the problem considering the same suite of factors. Starting with the people—instead of the technology—guides innovation investment toward solutions that ultimately will be adopted and embraced.

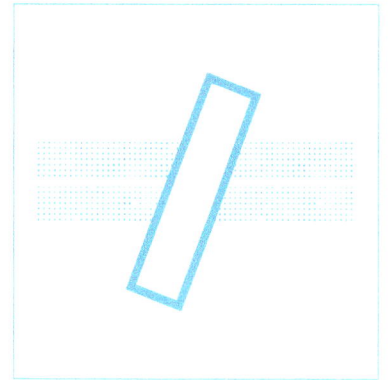

Pay Attention to Outliers

Existing policy and project design methodologies tend to rely on disciplines that favor quantitative data and are based on set assumptions about how beneficiaries react to certain interventions. The goal is to create universal models that explain behavior by focusing on similarities and discarding outliers.

Design thinking is different because it pays attention not only to similarities between people, but also to meaningful differences. This challenges the researcher to be mindful of their own confirmation bias, which happens when they unintentionally favor what fits the framework and accidentally ignore what does not. Outliers are the people that fall outside "normal," and are most often the ones who suffer when policy is designed for similarities instead of differences.

Paying attention to outliers challenges designers to reconsider what one-size-fits-all looks like. The brand OXO designs kitchen tools for people with arthritic hands so they can grip and use them more easily. Now, these ergonomic designs are broadly adopted in the industry because they are simply more comfortable for everyone.

Outliers provide inspiration by revealing ingenuity, hacks, and best practices that can have powerful impact when scaled. Oftentimes a solution that suits outliers will also work for the majority of others.

Data Gives You the What, Context Gives You the Why

In the past, organizations have put data and context in competition with one another for credibility. To policy and decision makers, quantitative data has been viewed as more credible and reliable. But without qualitative research, data often misses important context that demonstrates the nature of how policy affects beneficiaries. Qualitative research can make sense of important context—like culture, ethics, and psychology—in ways that quantitative fields do not.

Data help us understand the "what" of human behavior at scale, but does not give us insight into the "why." Qualitative research provides insights into "why" people do what they do,

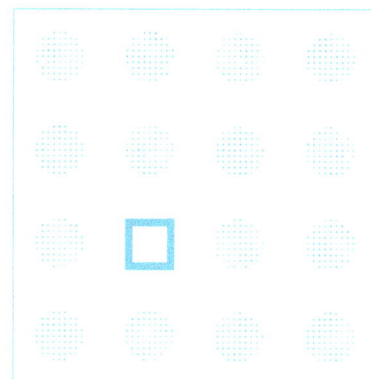

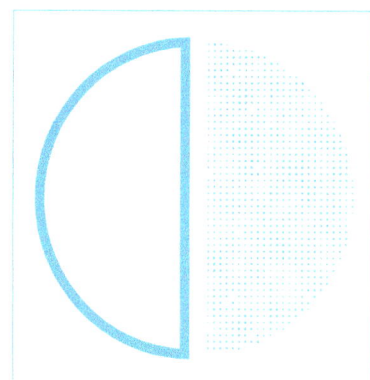

but does not measure the prevalence of these insights across populations. Blending data and context allows decision makers to see from multiple angles, making up for the blind spots inherent to each approach.

Policy makers need both the "what" and the "why," but how to combine them in practice is just beginning to be understood. In the private sector, human-centered designers are beginning to work with data scientists to identify broad patterns, understand their relevance, develop hypotheses that can inform a divergent set of solutions, and measure the impact of those solutions.

The Human Account, a collaboration between Dalberg Design and Rockefeller Philanthropy Advisors, shows how hybrid research can happen in the social sector.[12] Data scientists, behavioral economists, designers, documentarians, and business strategists worked in sequenced sprints to create new financial segments for six countries in Asia and Africa.

Insights from 76 ethnographic interviews formed the underlying contextual, behavioral, and psychometric variables for a global survey of 11,500 people. The resulting 35 clusters identified by the research instrument were enriched by documentary filmmakers who chronicled the lives of 35 different families or individuals representing each segment.

Measure Success from the Human Perspective

At the end of the day, success needs to be measured to know if policy objectives are achieved. Governments, organizations, and companies evaluate success very differently from the people they intend to serve. Institutional objectives are usually quantitative, while people perceive success qualitatively. The goal is for both types of success to align.

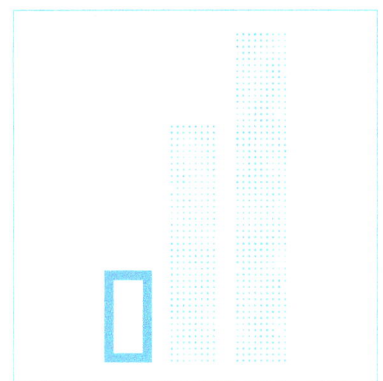

[12]   Dalberg's Design Impact Group. 2018. *The Human Account*. thehumanaccount.com.

While policy makers can look to data like enrollment figures, percentage of budget spent, teacher–pupil ratios, or Programme for International Student Assessment (PISA) scores, human perceptions around success are much more challenging to detect and measure. Human-centered design can help policy makers understand success from the human perspective—and create measures of success that reflect it—by first understanding how people define success for themselves: Is my child treated well in school? Will she find a good job? Can she go to college?

In another example, a health-care organization wanted to develop a new service to help people quit smoking. From qualitative research, they learned that "quitting" was not how end-users evaluate their own success; instead their objective was to "feel in control." This means that evaluation of the new service must include both quantitative and qualitative measurements: the number of people who quit and those who "feel a greater sense of control."

Finding ways to detect and monitor success, from the human perspective, aids decision makers in evaluating if policy is having the desired impact.

FEATURED FURTHER READING

The Human Account

Dalberg Design and Rockefeller Philanthropy Advisors

An 18-month research project focused on investigating the financial health of people in six developing countries (India, Kenya, Myanmar, Nigeria, Pakistan, and Tanzania). The project went public with the results in 2018. It is remarkable because of the way that human-centered design, behavioral economics, market research, and filmmaking were used in tandem to discover new financial segments that transcend demographics to include behavior and psychology.

Communicating the New

Kim Erwin

Communicating among stakeholders about innovation is very different from any other kind of communication. There is no precedent because what is being discussed is brand-new. The effectiveness with which learnings, thoughts, and recommendations are communicated directly relates to the innovation moving forward. This book is about how to explain innovation work—to ourselves, to our teammates, and to others—and how to engage others in advancing new ideas into organizations and markets. It offers methods that help manage complexity, accelerate synthesis, and clarify and diffuse important knowledge for the people who need to act on it.

The Convivial Toolbox

Liz Sanders and Pieter Jan Stappers

Generative design research is about bringing end-users and beneficiaries into the design process directly and using their creativity to understand needs and aspirations. This is an academic book that provides background on the evolution of this discipline and what makes it distinct from other types of research, such as participatory design. The bulk of the book, however, offers practical guidance on its application through underlying principles of generative design research, cases, and a how-to section.

The Policy Project

Government of New Zealand, Department of the Prime Minister and Cabinet

The Policy Project is a cross-agency team tasked with lifting policy quality and capability across the New Zealand Public Service. Through common frameworks, their goal is to improve consistency in the quality of policy advice, the skills of policy practitioners and the capability of policy organizations, and ultimately improve overall system capability. One of the tools they use, especially when confronting new issues when there is not existing data, is design thinking. They offer an overview, tools, articles, and resources on their website for other policy makers interested in using a similar human-centered approach.

Doing Development Differently

The DDD Manifesto Community. 2019. *Doing Development Differently.* https://buildingstatecapability.com/the-ddd-manifesto/.

The manifesto is a call to international development organizations of all kinds to embrace human-centered principles as the best way to address complex challenges and foster impact.

The content is developed by practitioners and researchers who implement these new development practices or carry out thorough analytical work on them.

FURTHER READING

Hall, E. 2018. *Thinking in Triplicate*. medium.com.

Heath, D. and C. Heath. 2010. *Switch: How to Change Things When Change Is Hard*. New York: Crown Business.

IDEO. 2011. *Human Centered Design Toolkit*. IDEO.org website. www.designkit.org/methods.

Junginger, S. 2017. *Human-centered Design and Public Sector Innovation*. Paris: Observatory of Public Sector Innovation, part of the Organisation for Economic Co-operation and Development. https://oecd-opsi.org/human-centered-design-and-public-sector-innovation-2/.

Kalil, T. 2015. *Using Human-centered Design to Make Government Work Better and Cost Less*. Obama White House Archives. https://obamawhitehouse.archives.gov/blog/2015/09/04/using-human-centered-design-make-government-work-better-and-cost-less.

Kelley, T. 2001. *The Art of Innovation*. New York: Harper Collins Business.

Kolko, J. 2015. Design Thinking Comes of Age. *Harvard Business Review*. September Issue. https://hbr.org/2015/09/design-thinking-comes-of-age.

Kumar, V. 2013. *101 Design Methods*. Hoboken: Wiley.

Lanchester, J. 2018. Can Economists and Humanists Ever Be Friends? *The New Yorker Magazine*. 16 July.

Lee, P. 2015. *Before The Backlash Let's Redefine User Centered Design*. Stanford: Stanford Social Innovation Review. 26 August.

Luetjens, J. 2016. *Design Thinking in Policymaking: Opportunities and Challenges*. Boston: Centre for Public Impact. www.centreforpublicimpact.org/design-thinking-in-policymaking/.

Merholz, P. and K. Skinner. 2016. *Org Design for Design Orgs.* Sebastopol: O'Reilly.

Morson, G. S. and M. Schapiro. 2017. *Cents and Sensibility.* Princeton: Princeton University Press.

Norman, D. 1988. *The Design of Everyday Things.* New York: Perseus Books.

Organisation for Economic Co-operation and Development (OECD). 2017. *Core Skills for Public Sector Innovation.* Paris: OECD. www.oecd.org.

Pulse Lab. 2016. *Augmenting Big Data: Haze Edition.* Jakarta: Pulse Lab. medium.com.

———. 2017. *Embracing Innovation: How a Social Lab Can Support the Change Agenda in Sri Lanka.* Jakarta: Pulse Lab. unglobalpulse.org.

Rankin, W. and J. Stanton. 2016. *Human-centered Design in Higher Education.* evolllution.com. https://evolllution.com/managing-institution/operations_efficiency/human-centered-design-in-higher-education/.

Szczepanska, J. 2017. *Design Thinking Origin Story Plus Some of the People Who Made It All Happen.* San Francisco. medium.com.

SOURCES

Anderson, K. 2009. Ethnographic Research: A Key to Strategy. *Harvard Business Review*. Vol. 87–3, March Issue. https://hbr.org/2009/03/ethnographic-research-a-key-to-strategy.

Dalberg's Design Impact Group. 2014. *Making the Case for Design in the Development Sector*. https://static1.squarespace.com/static/543bf912e4b067de38e4b116/t/547e0d6ae4b0e77baa73014f/1417547114314/Case_for_Design_in_the_Develoment_Sector.pdf.

———. 2018. *The Human Account*. https://www.thehumanaccount.com/.

Design for Health. 2019. Complementary Approaches. https://www.designforhealth.org/resources/complimentary-approaches-design-for-health.

Education Sector Analytical and Capacity Development Partnership (ACDP-026). 2017. *Preparing Skilled and Highly Skilled Manpower for Indonesia's Modernizing Maritime Sector*. Jakarta: ACDP.

Erwin, K. 2013. *Communicating the New: Methods to Shape and Accelerate Innovation*. Hoboken: Wiley.

Fabricant, R. 2014. When Will Design Get Serious About Impact? Stanford: Stanford Social Innovation Review. https://ssir.org/articles/entry/when_will_design_get_serious_about_impact.

Government of New Zealand. 2019. *The Policy Project*. Wellington: Department of the Prime Minister and Cabinet. https://dpmc.govt.nz//our-programmes/policy-project.

Keeley, L., R. Pikkel, H. Walters, and B. Quinn. 2013. *Ten Types of Innovation: The Discipline of Building Breakthroughs*. Hoboken: Wiley.

Sanders, L. and P. J. Stappers. 2013. *The Convivial Toolbox*. Amsterdam: BIS Publishers.

Serrat, O. 2010. *Design Thinking*. Manila: Asian Development Bank.

ABOUT THE AUTHORS

Jamie Munger has led human-centered projects in Canada, the People's Republic of China, Haiti, India, and the United States. She works with organizations in the public and private sectors, helping them develop offerings that demonstrate deep insight of end-user needs, aspirations, and lives. She founded and ran the Chicago-based innovation firm Emergent Design, as cofounder and principal. There she worked on in-depth human-centered design projects for clients, including Herman Miller, the University of Chicago, and Specialized Bikes. She coached start-ups using design thinking to develop product-market fit as designer-in-residence at the University of Chicago. Jamie also worked as designer at the outdoor clothing company, The North Face, a turning point in her evolving ideas about the importance of designing with the end-users in mind. She earned master's-level degrees in design methods and business administration from the Illinois Institute of Technology and holds a BA in sociology from Emory University. She lives in Brooklyn, New York.

Rudi Van Dael is an ADB specialist who has worked in the education sector in South and Southeast Asia. He and his colleagues administered the Education Sector Analytical and Capacity Development Partnership (ACDP) in 2017 when the study on maritime education and training was conducted. ACDP was a research facility financed by the Government of Australia and the European Union and administered by ADB. It supported the Government of Indonesia by conducting demand-led policy analysis, knowledge management, and capacity building in the education sector. ACDP supported various government agencies including the Ministry of Education and Culture, the Ministry of National Development Planning, the Ministry of Research, Technology, and Higher Education, and the Ministry of Religious Affairs. In total, 51 studies were prepared between 2011 and 2017.